United States Catholic Elementary and Secondary Schools 2016-2017

The Annual Statistical Report on Schools, Enrollment and Staffing

Dale McDonald, PBVM, Ph.D.

Margaret Schultz

NCEA
National Catholic Educational Association

Published in the United States of America by the National Catholic Educational Association.

www.NCEA.org

Part No. RES-55-1563
ISBN No. 978-1-55833-616-2

Table Of Contents

List of Exhibits

Preface

The National Catholic Educational Association (NCEA) has been providing leadership and service to Catholic education since 1904. Rooted in the Gospel of Jesus Christ, NCEA is a professional membership organization that assists its members to fulfill their teaching mission of the Church and to lead, learn and proclaim the good news of Catholic school education.

NCEA is the largest private professional association in the world, representing more than 150,000 educators serving almost 1.9 million students in preschool, elementary and secondary schools.

Since 1970, the NCEA has published a statistical report on Catholic elementary and secondary schools in the United States. These annual reports are designed to provide an understanding of this significant sector of American education, to inform the public discussion of educational policy issues and to encourage and improve practice at the school level.

The first part of this report presents data concerning an overview of the historical dimensions of Catholic education and the context of American education in which private schools operate. This is followed by Catholic school enrollment and staffing demographic data that highlight school, student and staffing characteristics and special services provided to students in Catholic schools.

The report is based upon census data gathered by each of the arch/diocesan offices of education in the United States, representing all 176 dioceses with Catholic schools. While every diocese is included, the data do not include responses to all of the items by all of the dioceses or by all the schools within each diocese.

We wish to thank the diocesan superintendents of schools and their staffs for their assistance in collecting and collating the data from their schools. Thank you also to Ms. Beatriz Ruiz, Graphic Designer at NCEA, and Jean Philippe Laplagne for production design.

Dale McDonald, PBVM, Ph.D.
Director of Public Policy and Educational Research

Margaret Schultz
Database Manager, NCEA Databank

Executive Summary

2016-2017 Academic Year

Catholic schools offer academic excellence and faith-filled education for students nationwide. National test scores, high school graduation rates, college attendance and other data show that Catholic schools frequently outperform schools in both the public and private sectors.

In the United States during the 2016-2017 academic year, 1,878,824 students were educated in 6,429 Catholic schools. 569,395 students attended 1,205 secondary schools and 1,309,429 students attended 5,224 elementary schools.

Enrollment figures for the 2016-2017 school year indicate that there are 37,012 fewer students, a 1.9 percent decrease from the previous academic year. At the same time there is a strong demand and enthusiasm for Catholic schools: Waiting lists now exist in 27% of the schools, primarily in suburban areas. Across the nation, 20 new schools opened this year and more are projected to open in the coming years.

Dioceses around the country are implementing successful programs of fundraising for tuition assistance, marketing, and academic and faith formation advancement. National initiatives are also in place to promote growth in Catholic school education and to address common issues which will prove to provide greater opportunity for parental choice.

In the public arena, 29 states and the District of Columbia have legislation that provides some form of financial assistance to parents to help them choose a private or faith-based education for their children. Currently there are 61 publicly-financed programs (vouchers, scholarships, education savings accounts and tax relief) assisting more than 1.5 million families with financial resources that enable them to exercise choice in their selection of a school for their children. Efforts are underway in several additional states to enact similar legislation.

There is growing optimism about parental choice as opinion polls continue to demonstrate rising support for publicly financed programs. However, there is still much more to do to assure that full and fair parental choice becomes a hallmark of education in this country.

Pope Benedict XVI, Address to Educators, April 17, 2008 Catholic University of America, Washington, DC: *"Education is integral to the mission of the Church to proclaim the Good News. First and foremost every Catholic educational institution is a place to encounter the living God who in Jesus Christ reveals his transforming love and truth... Those who meet him are drawn by the very power of the Gospel to lead a new life characterized by all that is beautiful, good and true...."* (cf. Spe Salvi, 4)

Highlights

Enrollment:

- Total Catholic school student enrollment for the current academic year is 1,878,824. 1,309,429 in elementary/middle schools; 569,395 in secondary schools
- Student diversity: 20.7% are racial minorities, 16.8% are Hispanic/Latino and 6.0% were reported as unknown in the racial data collection.
- Non-Catholic enrollment is 345,327 which is 18.4% of the total enrollment.

Schools:

- There are 6,429 Catholic schools: 5,224 elementary; 1,205 secondary.
- 20 new schools opened; 96 consolidated or closed.*
- 1,739 schools have a waiting list for admission.
- Coeducational schools comprise 98.6% of elementary and 70.0% of secondary schools. At the secondary level, 12.7% of the schools are male and 17.3% are female.

**The reported number of schools closed includes some that consolidated and re-opened as new entities. The total reported opened is 20 which includes newly built as well as the reconfigured entities. The net loss of elementary schools is 101 and the number of secondary schools is 5 greater than last year.*

Professional Staff:

- Full-time equivalent professional staff numbered 152,883:

97.4%: Laity	(Lay women: 75.3% Lay men: 22.1%)
2.6%: Religious/Clergy	(Sisters: 1.6%; Brothers: 0.5%; Clergy: 0.5%)

- The student/teacher ratio is 12:1.

Catholic School Education in Historical Perspective

The existence of Catholic schools in the United States can be traced back to French and Spanish settlements that continued into the colonial era of this nation's history. The increased immigration of Catholic populations in the 19th century produced an expansion of Catholic schooling.

In the 1830's, the public, "common" school movement was begun to serve distinct national social and political goals: a common body of knowledge was to be transmitted in a common schoolhouse in order to decrease political and social conflict and shape the culture of the new nation. However, by the 1840s, public education and the inculcation of religious values were bound together in a concept of non-denominational Christianity.

Catholics began to resist attempts to teach "common Christianity" and were embroiled in conflicts charged with religious, ethnic and class animosities over control of the schools. Ultimately, the Second Baltimore Council directly attacked the Protestantism of the common school and the Catholic bishops committed the Church to the establishment of a separate school system and required parents to send their children.

While the goal of erecting a school within every parish, mandated by the Third Plenary Council of Baltimore (1884), was never realized, the growth of Catholic education was steady and extraordinary. Before the Civil War, there were approximately 200 Catholic schools in the United States, and that number increased to more than 1,300 within a decade and to 5,000 by the turn of the century.

In the 20th century, constitutional battles were fought over compulsory public education and the liberty to choose alternatives. The Supreme Court legitimized a dual system of education (*Pierce v. Society of Sisters, 1925; Yoder v. Wisconsin, 1972*) with decisions that protected the right of the non-public school to exist and the freedom of parents to choose from among alternatives for their children. As these alternative systems began to reflect upon their service to the common good and examined the fiscal costs in providing such public service, they began to challenge the inequities inherent in denial of funding because of educational choices exercised by parents.

This debate continues today as part of the national conversation about educational reform and the rights of parents to determine the best educational setting for their children. The U.S. Supreme Court ruling in *Zelman v. Simmons-Harris* (2002) that allowed publicly funded vouchers to be used by parents to fund tuition in private and religious schools energized the parental school choice movement. Efforts to secure public financial support for low-income students to attend Catholic schools have met with modest success and are gaining momentum as new programs are created each year across the nation.

Parental choice in education continues to experience growth: 29 states and the District of Columbia offer 61 different voucher/scholarship, education savings accounts and tax credit programs that serve more than 1.5 million families who choose to send their children to faith-based or private schools or homeschool.

While there is optimism about additional legislation being enacted on the federal and state levels, there is still much to do to assure that full and fair parental choice becomes a hallmark of education in this country. The parental choice program gains enacted in some states have become a catalyst for others to energize people of good will to work for educational justice for all children, especially those of low and modest means.

Historical Enrollment and Staffing Patterns

Schools and Enrollment History

Exhibit 1 reports the steady growth of Catholic schools from 1920 to the mid-1960s. By 1965, the peak year, there were almost 13,000 schools enrolling 5.2 million students. The next two decades saw a significant diminishment in the both the numbers of schools and their enrollment. In the 1990s, the rate of school closures declined and total enrollment rose steadily. However, during the past decade, schools in the central cities have experienced sharp declines in enrollment due to down-turned economic trends, demographic changes in those areas and sharp increases in tuition rates. This decline impacted elementary schools primarily while secondary enrollment remained relatively stable until 2008 when secondary began a slow decline which never exceeded 1% in any year. In the 2016-2017 school year there has been a decline of 1.5% in secondary enrollment and 2.1% in elementary. Overall, the national enrollment decline since 2007 has been greater than 441,000, a 19.0% loss of the student population.

EXHIBIT 1: Schools and Enrollment History

	SCHOOLS			ENROLLMENT		
	Elementary	Secondary	Total	Elementary	Secondary	Total
1920	6,551	1,552	8,103	1,796,000	130,000	1,926,000
1930	7,923	2,123	10,046	2,223,000	242,000	2,465,000
1940	7,944	2,105	10,049	2,035,000	361,000	2,396,000
1950	8,589	2,189	10,778	2,561,000	506,000	3,067,000
1960	10,501	2,392	12,893	4,373,000	880,000	5,253,000
1970	9,366	1,986	11,352	3,359,000	1,008,000	4,367,000
1980	8,100	1,540	9,640	2,293,000	846,000	3,139,000
1990	7,395	1,324	8,719	1,983,000	606,000	2,589,000
2000	6,923	1,221	8,144	2,013,084	639,954	2,653,038
2010	5,889	1,205	7,094	1,507,618	611,723	2,119,341
2017	**5,224**	**1,205**	**6,429**	**1,309,429**	**569,395**	**1,878,824**

School Staffing History

During the last quarter of the 20th century, dramatic changes took place in the staffing of Catholic schools. The staffing patterns listed by decades in Exhibit 2 indicate the depth of the change. The data show the shift from an almost entirely religious staff (sisters, brothers, priests, deacons) of 90.1% at mid-century (1950) to 48.4% in the 1970s to a primarily lay staff, now at 97.4% during the current school year. In general, the changes have been attributed to the decline in the number of women and men entering religious orders, the large numbers of religious who left their orders and the change of ministry directions for many congregations from schools to other forms of social and pastoral ministries.

EXHIBIT 2: School Staffing History

FULL-TIME EQUIVALENT TOTAL STAFF

	RELIGIOUS		LAY		TOTAL
	Number	%	Number	%	
1920	45,563	92.0%	3,942	8.0%	49,505
1930	65,601	90.4%	6,951	9.6%	72,552
1940	73,960	91.2%	7,097	8.8%	81,057
1950	84,925	90.1%	9,370	9.9%	94,295
1960	112,029	73.8%	39,873	26.2%	151,902
1970	80,615	48.4%	85,873	51.6%	166,488
1980	42,732	29.0%	104,562	71.0%	147,294
1990	20,020	14.6%	116,880	85.4%	136,900
2000	11,011	7.0%	146,123	93.0%	157,134
2010	5,749	3.7%	148,567	96.3%	154,316
2017	**3,997**	**2.6%**	**148,886**	**97.4%**	**152,883**

TOTAL STAFF SUMMARY 2016 - 2017

Staff	Elementary/Middle	Secondary	Total
Female Religious	1,718	752	2,470
Male Religious	180	563	743
Clergy (priest/deacon)	261	523	784
Female Lay	87,196	27,914	115,110
Male Lay	11,530	22,246	33,776
Total	**100,885**	**51,998**	**152,883**

Teaching Staff	Number	Percentage
Lay	148,886	97.4%
Religious/Clergy	3,997	2.6%

Public/Private School Comparisons

Private schools, defined as those controlled by a non-governmental entity and financed from sources other than public taxation, have been an important component of American education since colonial days. The existence of private schools reflects the fundamental right of parents to exercise freedom of choice in selecting the education they deem most appropriate for their children. Parents select private schools based on several factors, among which are the religious, educational, cultural and social values that are espoused by the institution.

The National Center for Educational Statistics (NCES) survey of the private schools during the 2013-2014 school year [latest available data] indicates that there were 33,619 private elementary and secondary schools in the United States. Private schools account for 25.5% of all American schools. Private schools enroll approximately 4.6 million Pre-K-12 students, representing 8.4% of total elementary and secondary student enrollment in the United States.

Private schools are categorized as Catholic, other religious and non-sectarian. Catholic schools are classified as a) parochial, b) diocesan, c) private. The category 'other religious schools' is comprised of three typologies: a) schools identified as conservative Christian, b) schools affiliated with a specific religious national denomination, c) schools not aligned with a national denomination. Non-sectarian schools are a) regular, b) special emphasis, c) special education.

Schools which are classified as 'other religious' constitute 48.7% of private schools, Catholic schools represent 19.9% and non-sectarian 31.7%. In contrast to the number of schools, there is a higher percentage of students in Catholic schools, which enroll 41.3% of private school students while other religious schools enroll 37.4% and nonsectarian 21.3%.

EXHIBIT 3: Public/Private School Comparisons

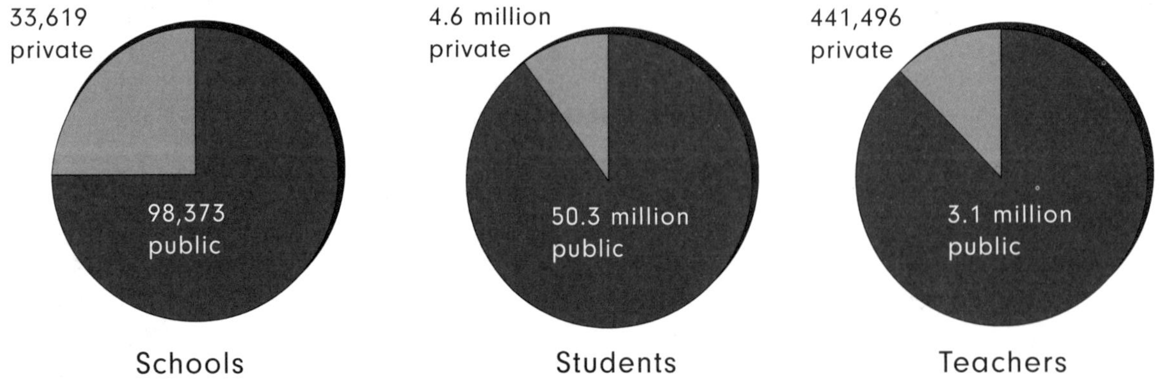

Sources: *Broughman, S.P. and Swaim, N.L. (2016); Glander, M. (2016).*

EXHIBIT 4: Comparisons of National Graduation Rates

Data collected from several sources by the U.S. Department of Education's National Center for Education Statistics (NCES) and the National Catholic Educational Association provide a portrait of American high school graduates and their post-secondary school experiences.

National Secondary School Graduation Rates

Type of School	Graduation Rate
Catholic	99.3%
Other Religious	97.8%
Non-Sectarian	95.2%
Public Schools	82.0% (actual high school diplomas awarded)

Sources: *Broughman, S.P. and Swaim, N.L. (2016), Kena, G et al. (2016).*

EXHIBIT 5: College Attendance Comparisons

The percentage of high school graduates who attend 4-year colleges:

Type of School	College Attendance Percentage*
Catholic	85.2%
Other Religious	63.3%
Non-Sectarian	56.2%
Public Schools	44%

*Data is not available for those attending community colleges, technical schools or enlistment in the military.

Sources: *BBroughman, S.P. and Swaim, N.L (2016); Kena, G. et al. (2016)*

EXHIBIT 6: Percentage Distribution of Private Schools by Enrollment Size

School Size	<50	50-149	150-299	300-499	500-749	750+
Catholic	5.8	23.4	38.8	19.0	8.5	4.5
Other Religious	56.1	24.0	11.7	4.5	2.1	1.5
Non-Sectarian	63.2	21.2	7.9	4.0	1.9	1.8

Sources: *Broughman, S.P. and Swaim, N.L (2016).*

Private School Universe

Some interesting changes have taken place within private education during the last 50 years. In 1965, Catholic education comprised approximately 68% of the schools and 87% of the enrollment in private education. At the start of the 21st century, religious schools of other denominations have grown rapidly and now comprise 48.7% of the private schools. They tend to be much smaller in size than Catholic schools, enrolling 37.3% of the students in nonpublic schools; Catholic schools comprise 19.9% of private schools, yet enroll 41.3% of the private school population. Non-Sectarian schools comprise 31.3% of the private schools and educate 21.3% of the students.

EXHIBIT 7: Percentage Distribution of Private Schools by Typology

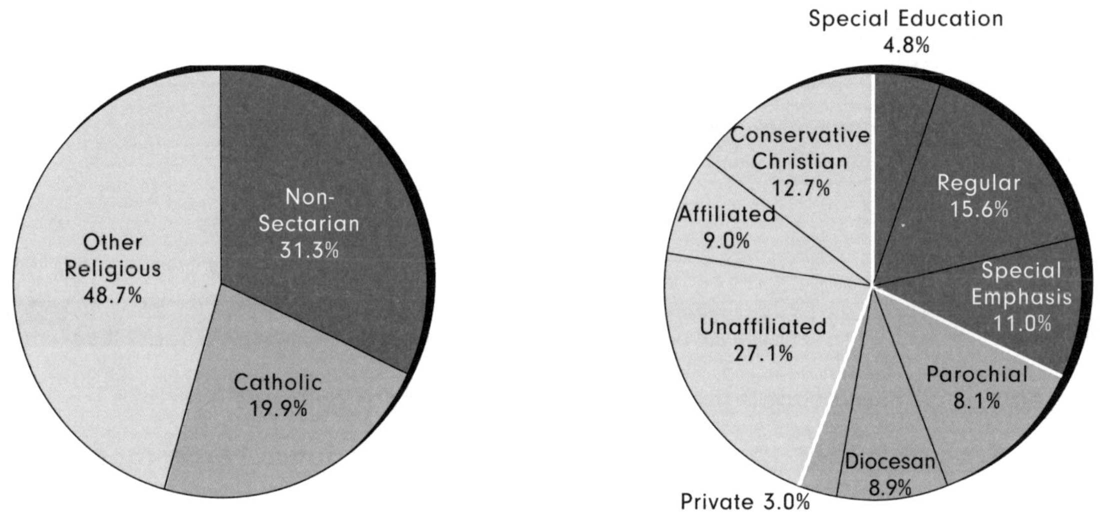

Sources: *Broughman, S.P. and Swaim, N.L (2016).*

EXHIBIT 8: Percentage Distribution of Students in Private Schools by Typology

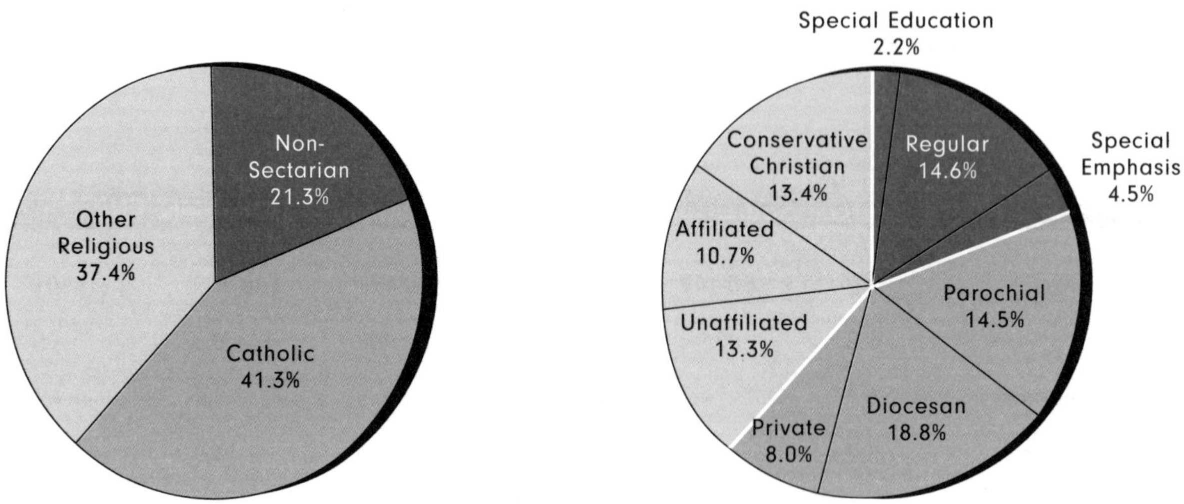

Sources: *Broughman, S.P. and Swaim, N.L (2016).*

Catholic School Demographics: 2016–2017 Academic Year

School Characteristics

Number of Schools

Elementary/Middle	Secondary	Total
5,224	1,205	6,429

Regional Distribution

Data are presented in regional groupings. For this purpose, the National Catholic Educational Association groups the schools and dioceses/archdioceses into the following six geographical regions:

New England

Connecticut
Maine
Massachusetts
New Hampshire
Rhode Island
Vermont

Great Lakes

Illinois
Indiana
Michigan
Ohio
Wisconsin

Southeast

Alabama
Arkansas
Florida
Georgia
Kentucky
Louisiana
Mississippi
North Carolina
South Carolina
Tennessee
Virginia
West Virginia

West/Far West

Alaska
Arizona
California
Colorado
Hawaii
Idaho
Montana
Nevada
New Mexico
Oklahoma
Oregon
Texas
Utah
Washington
Wyoming

Mideast

Delaware
District of Columbia
Maryland
New Jersey
New York
Pennsylvania

Plains

Iowa
Kansas
Minnesota
Missouri
Nebraska
North Dakota
South Dakota

Regional Distribution

Exhibit 9 presents the number of schools within each of the regions with the percentages of the distribution indicated by level of the schools and the national composite. Almost half of all the schools (45.2%) are located within the Mideast and Great Lakes regions. The national trend of population increases in the Southeast and West during the last decade is reflected in the school data. Overall, Catholic schools in those areas increased to 36.2% of the total as schools in New England, the Mideast and Great Lakes continued to experience closures.

EXHIBIT 9: Regional Distribution of Elementary/Middle and Secondary Schools

	2006-2007		2011-2012		2016-2017	
Elementary/Middle	**Number**	**%**	**Number**	**%**	**Number**	**%**
New England	411	6.5	331	5.9	301	5.8
Mideast	1,590	25.3	1,294	23.0	1,107	21.2
Great Lakes	1,547	24.6	1,386	24.6	1,267	24.3
Plains	745	11.8	701	12.4	668	12.8
Southeast	786	12.5	758	13.4	744	14.2
West/Far West	1,209	19.2	1,166	20.7	1,137	21.7
United States	**6,288**	**100.0**	**5,636**	**100.0**	**5,224**	**100.0**
Secondary						
New England	90	7.4	89	7.4	90	7.5
Mideast	316	26.1	300	24.9	290	24.1
Great Lakes	242	20.0	246	20.4	241	20.0
Plains	137	11.3	138	11.5	136	11.3
Southeast	183	15.1	190	15.8	197	16.3
West/Far West	242	20.0	242	20.0	251	20.8
United States	**1,210**	**100.0**	**1,205**	**100.0**	**1,205**	**100.0**
Totals of all Schools						
New England	501	6.7	420	6.1	391	6.1
Mideast	1,906	25.4	1,594	23.3	1,397	21.7
Great Lakes	1,789	23.9	1,632	23.9	1,508	23.5
Plains	882	11.8	839	12.3	804	12.5
Southeast	969	12.9	948	13.9	941	14.6
West/Far West	1,451	19.4	1,408	20.5	1,388	21.6
United States	**7,498**	**100.0**	**6,841**	**100.0**	**6,429**	**100.0**

Location of Schools

Although there has been a significant decrease in the total number of Catholic schools during the past four decades, the church has not lost sight of its commitment to educate children, particularly those of the poor, within the inner cities and urban areas. Schools in these areas remain a significant presence: four decades ago 47.9% were located in urban and inner city areas, today 40.4% of the schools are still in urban/inner city locales despite population losses and great financial difficulties in maintaining them. During that same period of time, suburban schools increased from 25.0% to 39.2% of the total.

EXHIBIT 10: Location of Schools 2016-2017

	Elementary		Secondary	
	Number	**%**	**Number**	**%**
Urban	1,526	29.3	439	36.3
Inner-City	508	9.7	119	9.9
Suburban	2,054	39.3	468	38.8
Rural	1,136	21.7	179	14.9
Total	**5,224**	**100.0**	**1,205**	**100.0**

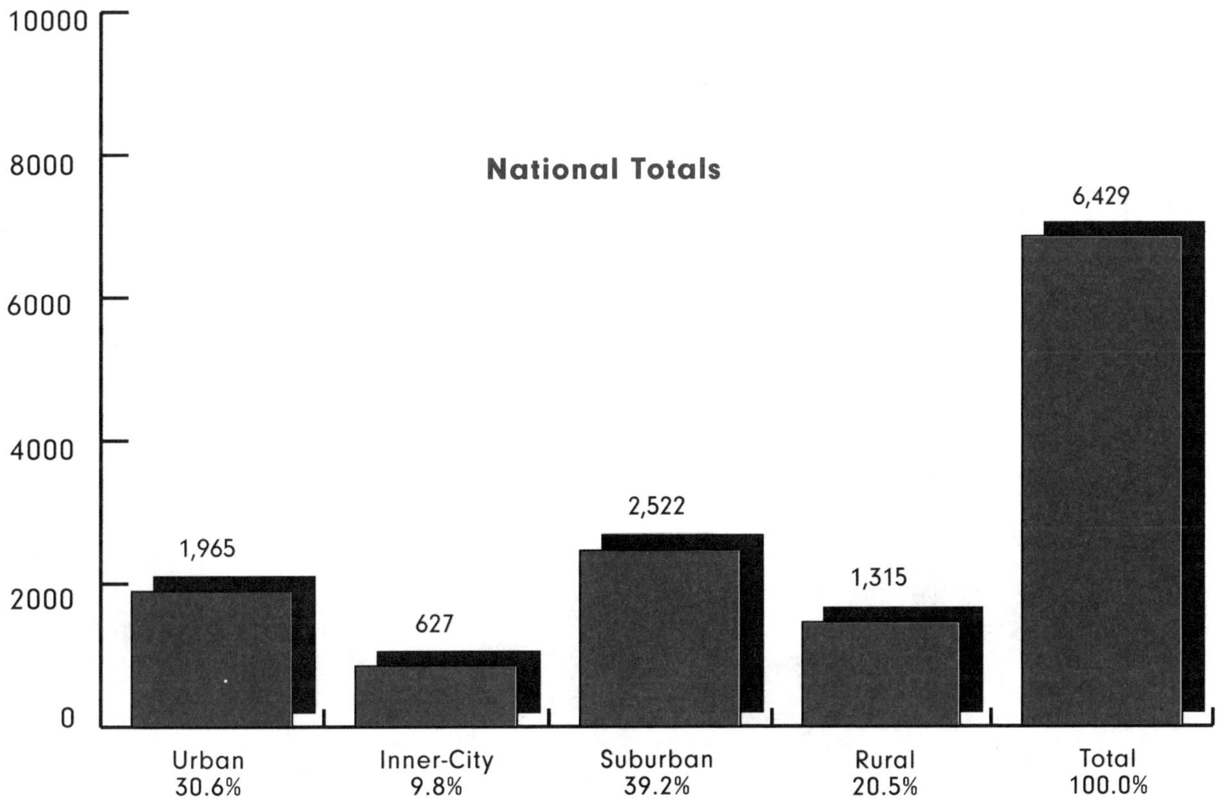

Types of Schools

Catholic school typologies are determined by the source of their sponsorship. There are four classifications of Catholic schools:

Parish: sponsored by a single parish church community

Inter-parish: sponsored by two or more parishes

Diocesan: sponsored by the arch/diocese

Private: sponsored by a religious order or a private corporation

Exhibit 11 indicates that most elementary schools are parish sponsored; however since 1990, the growth in the number and percentage of elementary inter-parish schools has risen from 8.9% in 1990 to 12.7% in 2017, reflecting the reorganization and consolidation of schools within dioceses. At the secondary level, sponsorship has remained fairly constant: private (45.1%) and diocesan (38.4%).

EXHIBIT 11: Schools by Types of Governance 2016-2017

	Elementary/Middle		Secondary	
	Number	**%**	**Number**	**%**
Parish	3,465	66.3	105	8.7
Inter-Parish	665	12.7	93	7.7
Diocesan	746	14.3	463	38.4
Private	348	6.7	544	45.1
Total	**5,224**	**100.0**	**1,205**	**100.0**

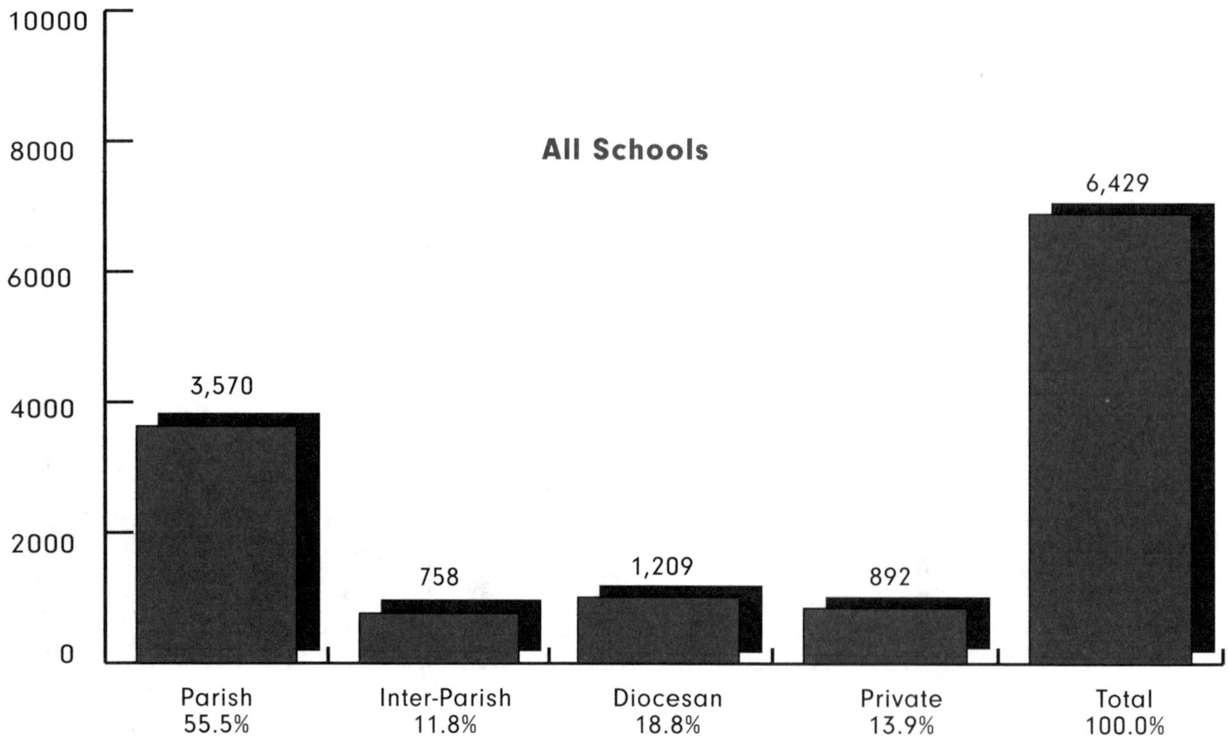

School Boards/Commissions/Councils

Over the past two decades, schools have continued to establish boards, councils or commissions to assist with school governance. Since 1994, when data were first collected, the percentage of schools with boards has increased from 14.3% to a current level of 84.1%. The 2016-2017 collection of data from Catholic schools revealed that of 6,429 schools, 5,404 reported having an existing school board, commission or council.

EXHIBIT 12: Schools with Boards/Commissions/Councils

Region	Number
New England	371
Mideast	1,126
Great Lakes	1,259
Plains	637
Southeast	823
West/Far West	1,188
Total	**5,404**

Single Gender Schools

The 2016-2017 data indicate that 1.4% of all Catholic elementary schools are single gender and 30.0% of secondary are single gender. Exhibit 13 illustrates their distribution.

EXHIBIT 13: Single Gender Schools

Region	Elementary Schools		Secondary Schools	
	Male	Female	Male	Female
New England	4	2	11	13
Mideast	17	15	53	79
Great Lakes	2	2	26	29
Plains	3	1	11	15
Southeast	5	8	22	27
West/Far West	6	8	30	46
Total	**37**	**36**	**153**	**209**

Total Single Gender	Number	Percent
Elementary/Middle	73	1.4% of elementary schools
Secondary	362	30.0% of secondary schools
Total Single Gender	**435**	**6.8% of all schools**

Single Gender Secondary Schools

Male: 12.7% of secondary schools

Female: 17.3% of secondary schools

School Openings and Consolidations/Closings

During the past school year, 20 new schools opened their doors. There were 96 schools that consolidated or closed.

EXHIBIT 14: School Openings/Closings/Consolidations

Region	Opened		Consolidated/Closed	
	Elementary	Secondary	Elementary	Secondary
New England	3	2	15	3
Mideast	2	0	21	1
Great Lakes	4	1	31	3
Plains	3	1	5	0
Southeast	0	3	5	1
West/Far West	0	1	11	0
National	**12**	**8**	**88**	**8**

School Enrollment

In this section, the data pertaining to enrollment in Catholic elementary and secondary schools are presented in several categories: grade levels, regional distributions, state and diocesan rankings and enrollment patterns.

EXHIBIT 15: Enrollment by Grade Level

	2006-2007		2011-2012		2016-2017	
Grade Level	Students	%	Students	%	Students	%
Preschool	152,429	9.1	154,282	10.6	169,000	12.7
Kindergarten	170,480	10.0	144,742	9.9	127,002	9.6
Grade 1	172,106	10.1	141,884	9.7	123,473	9.3
Grade 2	170,907	10.1	143,101	9.8	125,956	9.5
Grade 3	171,417	10.1	143,493	9.8	128,188	9.6
Grade 4	171,503	10.1	142,611	9.8	129,552	9.7
Grade 5	172,042	10.1	144,073	9.9	129,275	9.7
Grade 6	175,649	10.4	148,074	10.2	132,047	9.9
Grade 7	169,859	10.0	145,445	10.0	131,363	9.9
Grade 8	166,768	9.8	146,126	10.0	131,739	9.9
Ungraded	1,964	0.1	3,479	0.2	1,641	0.1
*Total Preschool - 8	1,697,124	100.0	1,457,310	100.0	1,329,236	100.0
Grade 9	164,211	26.3	149,017	26.0	136,263	24.8
Grade 10	156,629	25.1	143,882	25.1	138,800	25.3
Grade 11	152,944	24.5	140,449	24.5	137,649	25.0
Grade 12	148,793	23.9	138,943	24.2	133,791	24.3
Ungraded	950	0.2	1,854	0.3	3,085	0.6
*Total 9 - 12	623,527	100.0	574,145	100.0	549,588	100.0
Grand Total	**2,320,651**	**100.0**	**2,031,455**	**100.0**	**1,878,824**	**100.0**

** NB: Because some elementary schools have a ninth grade and some secondary schools have grades 6-8 in their totals, this distribution does not match that in Exhibits 16 and 26.*

Enrollment by Region

The national enrollment data, charted by region in Exhibit 16, show that the Mideast and Great Lakes regions enroll almost half the Catholic school population (45.6%). This percentage does indicate a decline from 49.8% over the past decade.

EXHIBIT 16: Enrollment by Region

	2006–2007		2011–2012		2016–2017	
Elementary/Middle	**Number**	**%**	**Number**	**%**	**Number**	**%**
New England	94,068	5.6	77,860	5.4	62,679	4.8
Mideast	447,571	26.6	336,356	23.3	283,156	21.6
Great Lakes	394,450	23.4	345,430	24.0	314,317	24.0
Plains	175,531	10.4	159,397	11.1	149,099	11.4
Southeast	254,437	15.1	228,883	15.9	220,557	16.8
West/Far West	316,355	18.8	292,646	20.3	279,621	21.4
United States	**1,682,412**	**100.0**	**1,440,572**	**100.0**	**1,309,429**	**100.0**
Secondary						
New England	46,810	7.3	41,944	7.1	39,636	7.0
Mideast	185,608	29.1	160,640	27.2	147,897	26.0
Great Lakes	127,905	20.0	118,518	20.1	112,376	19.7
Plains	54,663	8.6	52,451	8.9	50,642	8.9
Southeast	91,925	14.4	91,633	15.5	92,378	16.2
West/Far West	131,328	20.6	125,697	21.3	126,466	22.2
United States	**638,239**	**100.0**	**590,883**	**100.0**	**569,395**	**100.0**
All Schools						
New England	140,878	6.1	119,804	5.9	102,315	5.4
Mideast	633,179	27.3	496,996	24.5	431,053	22.9
Great Lakes	522,355	22.5	463,948	22.8	426,693	22.7
Plains	230,194	9.9	211,848	10.4	199,741	10.6
Southeast	346,362	14.9	320,516	15.8	312,935	16.7
West/Far West	447,683	19.3	418,343	20.6	406,087	21.6
United States	**2,320,651**	**100.0**	**2,031,455**	**100.0**	**1,878,824**	**100.0**

States with Highest School Enrollments

As detailed in Exhibit 17, ten states accounted for 60.5% of Catholic school enrollment. California, New York, Illinois, Ohio and Pennsylvania - the top five – had 40.6% of total enrollment.

EXHIBIT 17: Student Enrollment: States with Ten Highest Enrollments

State	2006-2007	2011-2012	2016-2017
California	235,011	214,139	207,925
New York	251,071	192,478	165,651
Illinois	170,165	151,815	135,456
Ohio	158,976	137,320	127,176
Pennsylvania	180,568	144,912	126,771
Florida	94,122	82,028	84,554
Louisiana	86,179	80,556	76,945
New Jersey	119,903	91,737	76,578
Texas	80,090	78,534	74,967
Missouri	75,039	66,605	59,838
10 Largest States	1,451,124	1,240,124	1,135,861
United States	2,320,651	2,031,455	1,878,824
Percent	62.5%	61.0%	60.5%

Dioceses with Largest Enrollments

The twenty largest dioceses serve 42.7% of the total enrollment in Catholic elementary and secondary schools, as illustrated in Exhibit 18. Many dioceses are larger than the metropolitan area of their title. Most of the enrollment in these 20 dioceses comes from the major city and the immediate suburbs of that area.

EXHIBIT 18: Student Enrollment: Dioceses with the Twenty Largest Enrollments

Diocese	2006-2007	2011-2012	2016-2017
Los Angeles	89,490	79,008	78,594
Chicago	98,225	86,502	76,095
New York	106,587	76,924	67,004
Philadelphia	96,257	76,894	66,638
Cleveland	55,394	46,903	43,159
Cincinnati	49,502	44,963	41,835
Brooklyn	57,405	45,213	38,264
St. Louis	50,019	43,005	38,220
Boston	47,366	41,964	37,547
New Orleans	40,955	37,826	35,330
Miami	37,666	33,906	33,884
Milwaukee	33,847	32,193	30,772
Newark	44,497	34,186	29,588
Detroit	38,252	32,841	29,224
St. Paul/Minneapolis	36,835	32,373	28,871
Washington, DC	31,971	27,928	26,856
Rockville Centre	34,885	30,824	26,350
Baltimore	34,972	27,962	25,105
San Francisco	26,460	24,416	24,566
Indianapolis	———	———	23,469
Seattle	———	22,754	———
Pittsburgh	24,368	———	———
20 Largest Dioceses	**1,034,953**	**878,585**	**801,371**
All Dioceses	**2,320,651**	**2,031,455**	**1,878,824**
Percent of enrollment	**44.6%**	**43.2%**	**42.7%**

EXHIBIT 19: Diocesan Enrollment Patterns

Total School Enrollment	Number of Dioceses	%
Fewer than 6,000	83	47.2
6,000 - 11,999	44	25.0
12,000 - 23,999	30	17.0
24,000 - 43,999	15	8.5
44,000 - 80,000	4	2.3

National Catholic School Trend Data

U. S. Catholic school enrollment reached its peak during the early 1960s when there were more than 5.2 million students in almost thirteen thousand schools across the nation. The 1970s and 1980s saw a steep decline in both the number of schools and students. By 1990, there were approximately 2.5 million students in 8,719 schools. From the mid 1990s though 2000, there was a steady enrollment increase (1.3%) despite continued closings of schools.

In the 10 years since the 2007 school year, 1,395 schools were reported closed or consolidated (18.6%), while 297 school openings were reported. Due to different definitions used by dioceses for consolidations, closings and their transitions into new configurations, along with actual new schools opened, the actual decrease in number of schools since 2007 is 1,069 schools (14.3%). The number of students declined by 441,827 (19.0%). The most seriously impacted have been elementary schools.

Exhibit 20 details the reported school closures. While the reported closures in the twelve large urban areas of the country is 434 over the past decade, the actual decrease in number of elementary schools in those dioceses since 2007 is 383 schools (18.2%). This is due to the same reasons stated above for the overall numbers.

There has been some good news as well during the 2007-2017 period as 297 new schools opened in all parts of the country. (Exhibit 21).

Exhibit 22 presents the national and elementary enrollment trend data. Since 2007, elementary school enrollment has declined by 27.7% in the 12 urban dioceses and 19.6% in the rest of the U.S.

(The twelve urban dioceses for this purpose are: Chicago, Philadelphia, New York, Los Angeles, Brooklyn, Cleveland, St. Louis, Newark, Boston, Cincinnati, New Orleans, Detroit)

EXHIBIT 20: National Catholic School Closures 2008-2017

Catholic School Closures/Consolidations 2008-2017 as reported by the dioceses

	2008	2009	2010	2011	2012	2013	2014	2015	2016	2017	Total 2008-2017
National	169	162	174	172	167	148	133	88	86	96	1395
Urban 12	39	56	46	51	65	73	67	37	24	28	486
National Minus Urban 12	130	106	128	121	102	75	66	51	62	68	909

Catholic Elementary School Closures/Consolidations 2008-2017 as reported by the dioceses

	2008	2009	2010	2011	2012	2013	2014	2015	2016	2017	Total 2008-2017
National	156	154	161	157	154	143	111	82	81	88	1287
Urban 12	35	52	42	44	54	70	56	33	23	25	434
National Minus Urban 12	121	102	119	113	100	73	55	49	58	63	853

EXHIBIT 21: National Catholic School Openings 2008-2017

Region	**2008**	**2009**	**2010**	**2011**	**2012**	**2013**	**2014**	**2015**	**2016**	**2017**	**2008-2017**
New England	6	1	2	3	0	2	0	0	2	5	21
Mideast	11	8	8	19	20	10	10	16	2	2	106
Great Lakes	6	7	3	5	4	7	17	2	2	5	58
Plains	6	4	0	1	5	5	5	2	2	4	34
Southeast	7	4	4	1	3	3	5	3	3	3	36
West/Far West	7	7	7	5	2	1	5	4	3	1	42
National	**43**	**31**	**24**	**34**	**34**	**28**	**42**	**27**	**14**	**20**	**297**

EXHIBIT 22: National Catholic School Enrollment Increases and Declines Trend Data 2007-2017

Total Enrollment

	2007	2009	2011	2013	2015	2017
National	2,320,651	2,192,531	2,065,872	2,001,740	1,939,574	1,878,824
Urban 12	773,949	710,466	658,568	630,852	609,333	581,498
National minus Urban 12	1,546,702	1,482,065	1,407,304	1,370,888	1,330,241	1,297,326

Chart of Percent Change in Total Enrollment 2007-2017

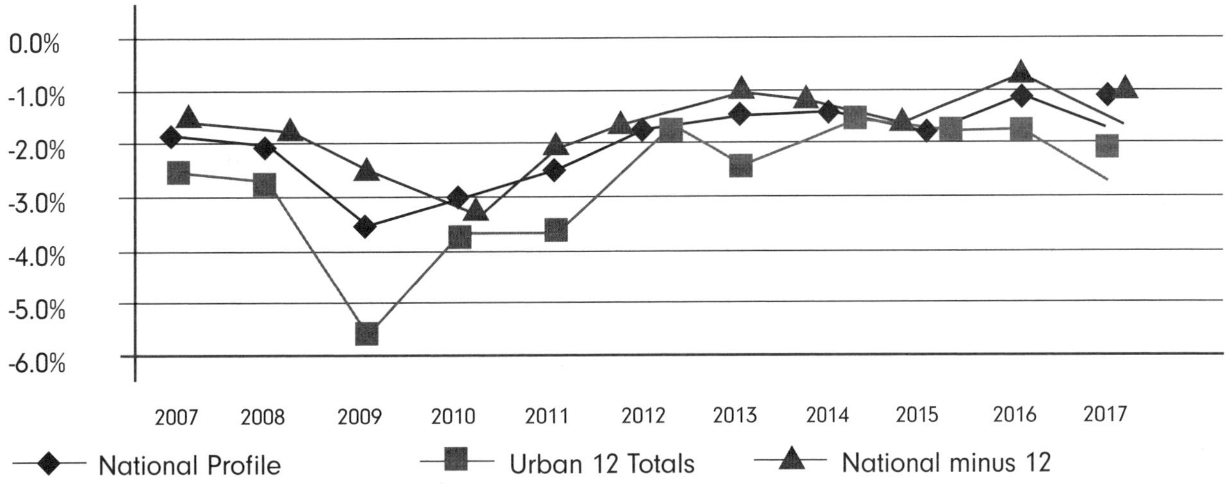

Elementary Enrollment

	2007	2009	2011	2013	2015	2017
National	1,682,412	1,568,016	1,467,694	1,415,244	1,359,969	1,309,429
Urban 12	539,732	487,787	447,170	428,138	411,504	390,414
National minus Urban 12	1,142,680	1,112,159	1,080,229	987,106	948,465	919,015

Chart of Percent Change in Elementary Enrollment 2007-2017

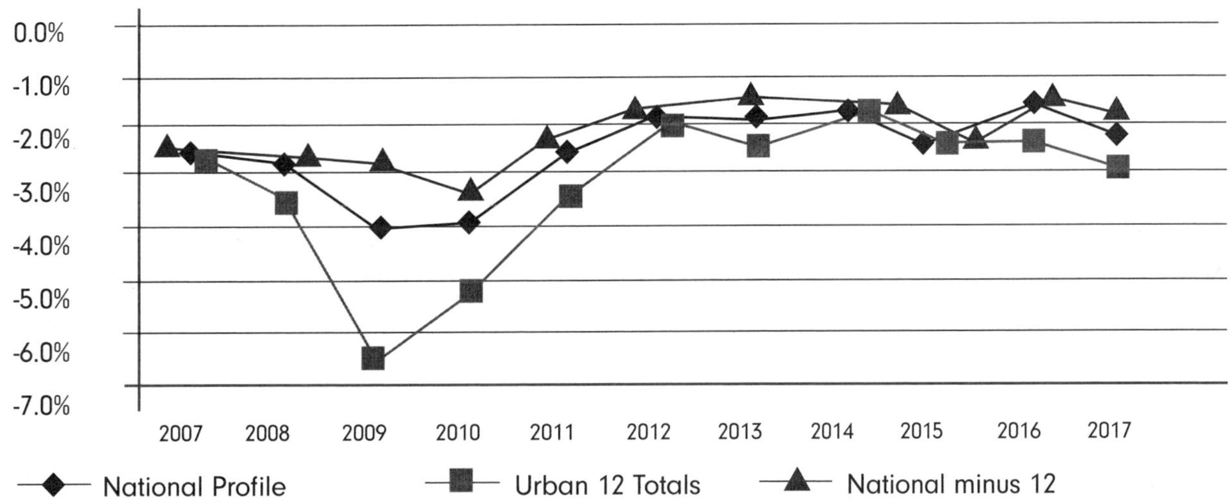

Schools with Waiting Lists

In spite of declining enrollments and school closures and consolidations, 27.0% of the schools have to place students on waiting lists for admissions.

EXHIBIT 23: Schools with Waiting Lists

	Number of Schools	Percentage in Region
New England	138	35.3%
Mideast	387	27.7%
Great Lakes	308	20.4%
Plains	120	14.9%
Southeast	370	39.3%
West/Far West	416	30.0%
Total	**1,739**	**27.0% of all schools**

Tuition and Costs

Tuition fees paid by families constitute a portion of the actual per pupil expenses. The average per pupil tuition in parish elementary schools is $4,400 which is approximately 74.7% of actual costs per pupil of $5,887. About 91% of elementary schools provide some form of tuition assistance.

The secondary mean freshman tuition is $9,840 which is approximately 70.6% of actual costs per pupil of $13,939. About 85% of secondary schools provide some form of tuition assistance.

The difference between the per pupil cost and the tuition charged is obtained in many ways, primarily through direct subsidy from parish, diocesan or religious congregation resources and from multi-faceted development programs and fund-raising activities.

EXHIBIT 24: Average Tuition and Per Pupil Costs

Elementary

Mean parish school tuition:	$4,400	Per pupil cost: $5,887

Secondary

Mean freshman tuition:	$9,840	Per pupil cost: $13,939

Based on the average public school per pupil cost of $11,066 Catholic schools provide more than 20 billion dollars a year savings for the nation. The published public school per pupil cost combines elementary and secondary pupils and ranges from $6,546 to more than $20,000.

Sources: *Kramarek, M. J., Gray, M.M., and McDonald, D. (2016), Cornman, S.Q. and Zhou, L. (2016)*

Diocesan Education Office Structures and Personnel

Each diocese determines its own organizational structure regarding the administration of Catholic educational ministries in school and catechetical programs. Although variations in titles occur across dioceses, the three general categories of administrative leadership are these:

- **Vicar for Education** or **Secretary for Education:** Member of the diocesan staff who serves as the representative of the bishop in the coordination of the educational ministries of the diocese.
- **Superintendent of Schools:** Member of the diocesan staff responsible for the educational ministry of the diocese as it is exercised in the Catholic schools.
- **Diocesan Director of Religious Education:** Member of the diocesan staff responsible for promoting the catechetical ministry in the diocese as it is exercised in its parish programs and schools.

The figures below indicate regional data regarding the personnel staffing the diocesan education offices. Many dioceses operated with very limited personnel: 19 education offices are staffed only by the superintendent and an additional 43 are staffed by a superintendent and one support person.

EXHIBIT 25: Diocesan Education Office Structures and Personnel

Region	Vicar for Education	Super-intendent	Diocesan Director of Religious Education	Assistant Super-intendent	Additional Professional Staff	Support Personnel	Total
New England	2	11	8	14	13	21	69
Mideast	11	24	17	66	109	65	292
Great Lakes	5	28	22	47	95	60	257
Plains	7	21	12	18	34	42	134
Southeast	10	33	24	39	42	56	204
West	6	50	27	52	67	71	273
Total	**41**	**167**	**110**	**236**	**360**	**315**	**1,229**

National Number of Staff with Combined Positions

Vicar/Secretary of Education, Superintendent, and DDRE:	3
Vicar/Secretary of Education and Superintendent:	11
Vicar/Secretary of Education and DDRE:	3
Superintendent and DDRE:	7

Distributions of Diocesan Office Personnel

	Number of Diocesan Offices	Number of Schools	Total Office Personnel
New England	11	391	69
Mideast	24	1,397	292
Great Lakes	29	1,508	257
Plains	25	804	134
Southeast	34	941	204
West	49	1,388	273
Total	**172**	**6,429**	**1,229**

Student Characteristics

Student Racial and Ethnic Diversity

Beginning with the 2012 data collection, NCEA adopted the federal standards for collecting and reporting demographic data in two categories: race and ethnicity. These federal standards mandate that race and Hispanic origin (ethnicity) are separate and distinct concepts and that when collecting these data two different questions must be used. Consequently, race and ethnic diversity will be reported in two separate exhibits.

Student diversity in Catholic schools has increased significantly in the past 40 years. When data were first collected, the Hispanic/Latino population was included and the reports listed non-Whites as "minorities." In 1970, the diversity percentage was 10.8%, in 1980 it had increased to 19.4% and by 2010 was 29.8%. In 2017, the racial diversity is 20.7% and Hispanic/Latino is 16.8%. NCEA will no longer use the minority identifier, but instead report racial and ethnic diversity separately.

EXHIBIT 26a: Catholic School Enrollment and Percentages by Race

	Elementary/Middle		Secondary		All Schools	
	Number	**%**	**Number**	**%**	**Number**	**%**
New England						
American Indian/Native Alaskan	90	0.1%	72	0.2%	162	0.2%
Asian	3,470	5.5%	3,214	8.1%	6,684	6.5%
Black	5,864	9.4%	2,418	6.1%	8,282	8.1%
Native Hawaiian/Pacific islander	101	0.2%	43	0.1%	144	0.1%
Multiracial	3,956	6.3%	1,333	3.4%	5,289	5.2%
White	48,464	77.3%	30,604	77.2%	79,068	77.3%
Unknown	734	1.2%	1,952	4.9%	2,686	2.6%
Total	**62,679**	**100.0%**	**39,636**	**100.0%**	**102,315**	**100.0%**
Mideast						
American Indian/Native Alaskan	725	0.3%	351	0.2%	1,076	0.2%
Asian	16,127	5.7%	9,038	6.1%	25,165	5.8%
Black	36,240	12.8%	18,659	12.6%	54,899	12.7%
Native Hawaiian/Pacific islander	1,031	0.4%	420	0.3%	1,451	0.3%
Multiracial	16,574	5.9%	6,345	4.3%	22,919	5.3%
White	196,331	69.3%	100,113	67.7%	296,444	68.8%
Unknown	16,128	5.7%	12,971	8.8%	29,099	6.8%
Total	**283,156**	**100.0%**	**147,897**	**100.0%**	**431,053**	**100.0%**
Great Lakes						
American Indian/Native Alaskan	3,525	1.1%	558	0.5%	4,083	1.0%
Asian	8,437	2.7%	3,931	3.5%	12,368	2.9%
Black	21,979	7.0%	11,041	9.8%	33,020	7.7%
Native Hawaiian/Pacific islander	539	0.2%	414	0.4%	953	0.2%
Multiracial	16,145	5.1%	4,186	3.7%	20,331	4.8%
White	250,300	79.6%	88,389	78.7%	338,689	79.4%
Unknown	13,392	4.3%	3,857	3.4%	17,249	4.0%
Total	**314,317**	**100.0%**	**112,376**	**100.0%**	**426,693**	**100.0%**

	Elementary/Middle		Secondary		All Schools	
	Number	%	Number	%	Number	%
Plains						
American Indian/Native Alaskan	1,279	0.8%	196	0.4%	1,475	0.7%
Asian	4,002	2.7%	1,842	3.6%	5,844	2.9%
Black	5,422	3.6%	2,442	4.8%	7,864	3.9%
Native Hawaiian/Pacific islander	333	0.2%	142	0.3%	475	0.2%
Multiracial	3,880	2.6%	1,345	2.6%	5,225	2.6%
White	128,227	85.2%	43,238	84.1%	171,465	84.9%
Unknown	7,431	4.9%	2,193	4.3%	9,624	4.8%
Total	**149,099**	**100.0%**	**50,642**	**100.0%**	**199,741**	**100.0%**
Southeast						
American Indian/Native Alaskan	1,178	0.5%	322	0.3%	1,500	0.5%
Asian	7,737	3.5%	3,106	3.4%	10,843	3.5%
Black	19,118	8.7%	8,453	9.2%	27,571	8.8%
Native Hawaiian/Pacific islander	619	0.3%	187	0.2%	806	0.3%
Multiracial	11,953	5.4%	3,296	3.6%	15,249	4.9%
White	177,784	80.6%	75,870	82.1%	253,654	81.1%
Unknown	2,168	1.0%	1,144	1.2%	3,312	1.1%
Total	**220,557**	**100.0%**	**92,378**	**100.0%**	**312,935**	**100.0%**
West/Far West						
American Indian/Native Alaskan	5,239	1.9%	1,308	1.0%	6,547	1.6%
Asian	27,489	9.8%	14,372	11.4%	41,861	10.3%
Black	8,297	3.0%	6,222	4.9%	14,519	3.6%
Native Hawaiian/Pacific islander	4,718	1.7%	2,754	2.2%	7,472	1.8%
Multiracial	31,263	11.2%	12,377	9.8%	43,640	10.7%
White	163,984	58.6%	75,492	59.7%	239,476	59.0%
Unknown	38,631	13.8%	13,941	11.0%	52,572	12.9%
Total	**279,621**	**100.0%**	**126,466**	**100.0%**	**406,087**	**100.0%**
National						
American Indian/Native Alaskan	12,259	0.9%	2,940	0.5%	15,199	0.8%
Asian	67,214	5.1%	35,687	6.3%	102,901	5.5%
Black	97,043	7.4%	49,437	8.7%	146,480	7.8%
Native Hawaiian/Pacific islander	7,297	0.6%	3,896	0.7%	11,193	0.6%
Multiracial	83,920	6.4%	28,847	5.1%	112,767	6.0%
White	964,981	73.7%	412,801	72.5%	1,377,782	73.3%
Unknown	76,715	5.9%	35,787	6.3%	112,502	6.0%
Total	**1,309,429**	**100.0%**	**569,395**	**100.0%**	**1,878,824**	**100.0%**

Hispanic/Latino Enrollment and Percentages

Federal guidelines require the identification of two ethnicities: Hispanic/Latino and Not Hispanic/Latino. Hispanic origin can be viewed as the heritage, nationality group, lineage, or country of birth of the person or ancestors before their arrival in the United States. People who identify their origin as Hispanic, Latino, or Spanish may be of any race. The Hispanic/Latino population is 16.8%

EXHIBIT 26b: Hispanic/Latino Enrollment and Percentages

	Elementary/Middle		Secondary		All Schools	
	Number	% in Region	Number	% in Region	Number	% in Region
New England	6,231	9.9%	2,693	6.8%	8,924	8.7%
Mideast	41,477	14.6%	15,739	10.6%	57,216	13.3%
Great Lakes	39,991	12.7%	12,275	10.9%	52,266	12.2%
Plains	12,098	8.1%	3,693	7.3%	15,791	7.9%
Southeast	35,249	16.0%	15,136	16.4%	50,385	16.1%
West/Far West	97,106	34.7%	33,922	26.8%	131,028	32.3%
Total	**232,152**	**17.7%**	**83,458**	**14.7%**	**315,610**	**16.8%**

Enrollment of Non-Catholics

Most Catholic school students are Catholic. However, non-Catholic student enrollment has risen from 2.7% in 1970 to 11.2% a decade later and today is 18.4% as shown in Exhibit 27.

EXHIBIT 27: Non-Catholic Enrollment

	Elementary/Middle		Secondary		All Schools	
	Number	% in Region	Number	% in Region	Number	% in Region
New England	12,841	20.5%	9,391	23.7%	22,232	21.7%
Mideast	58,922	20.8%	32,607	22.0%	91,529	21.2%
Great Lakes	49,230	15.7%	22,888	20.4%	72,118	16.9%
Plains	19,324	13.0%	7,422	14.7%	26,746	13.4%
Southeast	38,513	17.5%	19,851	21.5%	58,364	18.7%
West/Far West	38,093	13.6%	36,245	28.7%	74,338	18.3%
United States	**216,923**	**16.6%**	**128,404**	**22.6%**	**345,327**	**18.4%**

National Totals	**Number**	**%**
Catholic	1,492,799	79.5%
Non-Catholic	345,327	18.4%
Not Reported	40,698	2.2%
Total	**1,878,824**	**100.0%**

Staffing of Catholic Schools

In 2016-2017, the total, full-time equivalent (FTE) teaching staff in Catholic elementary/middle and secondary schools is 152,883.

The FTE represents the total of all the full-time professional staff and each of the part-time professional staff weighted as 0.333.

Per pupil ratios: The pupil/teacher ratio in Catholic schools in 2016-2017, determined by the FTE, was approximately 12:1. By level they are: elementary/middle schools: 13:1, secondary schools: 11:1.

Over the past decade, the lay faculty percentages increased from 93% to the current 97.4%. At present, 2.6% of the professional staff are religious and clergy. Exhibit 28 presents the FTE data by category and percentage.

Racial, ethnic and religious background data regarding all of the professional staff were collected. Exhibit 30 details the numbers and percentages of the religious background of the professional staff members and Exhibit 31 provides the racial and ethnic profiles and percentages of the professional staff.

EXHIBIT 28: Full-time Equivalent Professional Staff 2016-2017

	Elementary	%	Secondary	%	All Schools	%	Total	%
Sisters	1,718	1.7	752	1.4	2,470	1.7	Lay	97.4
Brothers	180	0.2	563	1.1	743	0.5	Religious/Clergy	2.6
Clergy	261	0.3	523	1.0	784	0.5		
Female Lay	87,196	86.4	27,914	53.7	115,110	75.3		
Male Lay	11,530	11.4	22,246	42.8	33,776	22.0		
***Total**	**100,885**	**100.0**	**51,998**	**100.0**	**152,883**	**100.0**		

**Adjusted totals to reflect weighted averages.*

EXHIBIT 29: Student/Teacher Ratio

Elementary	**13:1**
Secondary	**11:1**
National	**12.1**

Religious Background

EXHIBIT 30: Faculty Religious Background*

	Elementary/Middle		Secondary		All Schools	
	Number	%	Number	%	Number	%
Catholic Faculty						
Region						
New England	5,433	89.6%	3,158	73.6%	8,591	83.0%
Mideast	21,881	84.7%	11,381	78.4%	33,262	82.4%
Great Lakes	23,834	87.0%	8,215	78.7%	32,049	84.7%
Plains	10,962	86.0%	3,789	73.4%	14,751	82.4%
Southeast	16,663	82.9%	6,823	76.2%	23,486	80.8%
West/Far West	20,215	85.8%	8,517	69.5%	28,732	80.2%
United States	**98,988**	**85.6%**	**41,883**	**75.3%**	**140,871**	**82.2%**
Non-Catholic Faculty						
Region						
New England	538	8.9%	711	16.6%	1,249	12.1%
Mideast	2,338	9.1%	2,138	14.7%	4,476	11.1%
Great Lakes	3,150	11.5%	2,053	19.7%	5,203	13.8%
Plains	1,525	12.0%	1,092	21.1%	2,617	14.6%
Southeast	2,989	14.9%	2,067	23.1%	5,056	17.4%
West/Far West	2,979	12.6%	3,357	27.4%	6,336	17.7%
United States	**13,519**	**11.7%**	**11,418**	**20.5%**	**24,937**	**14.6%**

National Totals	**Number**	**%**
Catholic	140,871	82.2%
Non-Catholic	24,937	14.6%
Not reported	5,519	3.2%
Total	**171,327**	**100.0%**

**Includes all full-time and part-time professional staff.*

EXHIBIT 31: Faculty Diversity: Numbers* and Percentages by Race and Ethnicity

	Elementary		Secondary		All Schools	
	Number	%	Number	%	Number	%
Race						
American Indian/Native Alaskan	382	0.3%	170	0.3%	552	0.3%
Asian	1,727	1.5%	988	1.8%	2,715	1.6%
Black	2,594	2.2%	1,472	2.6%	4,066	2.4%
Native Hawaiian/Pacific Islander	493	0.4%	297	0.5%	790	0.5%
Multiracial	2,362	2.0%	945	1.7%	3,307	1.9%
White	102,976	89.0%	48,804	87.8%	151,780	88.6%
Unknown	5,186	4.5%	2,931	5.3%	8,117	4.7%
Total	**115,720**	**100.0%**	**55,607**	**100.0%**	**171,327**	**100.0%**
Ethnicity						
Hispanic	10,572	9.1%	4,029	7.2%	14,601	8.5%
Non-Hispanic	105,148	90.9%	51,578	92.7%	156,726	91.5%

**Includes all full-time and part-time professional staff.*

Special Services to Students

Extended Day Programs

The 2016-2017 data collection of Catholic elementary and middle schools revealed that of all schools reporting this information, 4,283 had extended day programs involving before and/or after school activities. This represents 82.0% of elementary/middle schools.

EXHIBIT 32: Schools with Extended Day Programs

Region	Number
New England	245
Mideast	984
Great Lakes	975
Plains	413
Southeast	671
West/Far West	995
Total	**4,283**

Serving Students with Special Needs

According to the most recent National Center for Education Statistics, 78.4 percent of Catholic schools serve students with mild to moderate special needs. These needs include physical, emotional and learning disabilities that are accommodated in regular classrooms with or without special resource teachers. The 2016-2017 data collection indicates that 4.6 percent of students in Catholic schools have a diagnosed disability. Exhibit 33 shows the number of students with special needs in each of the regions of the country.

EXHIBIT 33: Students with Special Needs

Region	Number
New England	3,482
Mideast	25,882
Great Lakes	10,242
Plains	11,004
Southeast	22,691
West/Far West	13,863
Total	**87,164**

Title I Services

NCEA data collection on the number of students receiving remedial instruction through Title I of the Elementary and Secondary Education Act (ESEA), formerly known as the No Child Left Behind Act (NCLB), are presented in Exhibit 34. The totals are lower than actual because several of the dioceses with large numbers of participating students have not supplied these data. A listing by region and state is found in Appendix F.

EXHIBIT 34: Students Receiving Title I Services

Region	Number of Schools	Students Receiving Services
New England	191	5,053
Mideast	746	33,915
Great Lakes	955	27,121
Plains	425	6,278
Southeast	464	17,294
West/Far West	685	24,014
Total	**3,466**	**113,675**

Federal Nutrition Programs

The 2016-2017 data collection reveals that many schools participate in the federal nutrition programs that provide free or reduced price breakfast and/or lunch to students whose family income level meets established criteria. The number of students receiving such services is indicated in Exhibit 35. The totals are lower than actual because several of the dioceses with large numbers of participating students have not supplied these data. A listing by region and state is found in Appendix F.

EXHIBIT 35: Participation in Federal Nutrition Programs

Region	Schools That Offer Program	Students Receiving Services	
		Breakfast	Lunch
New England	132	6,796	8,522
Mideast	467	39,436	47,484
Great Lakes	1,035	32,123	62,960
Plains	571	7,655	34,644
Southeast	343	16,998	23,398
West/Far West	423	19,530	32,393
Total	**2,971**	**122,538**	**209,401**

Government Subsidized/Free Transportation to School

Many dioceses reported that students were provided free or subsidized transportation services to/from school by local or state governments. The number of students reported receiving such services is indicated in Exhibit 36. Not all dioceses have provided this information. A listing by region and state is found in Appendix F.

EXHIBIT 36: Students Receiving Government Subsidized/Free Transportation to School

Region	Schools	Number
New England	158	7,739
Mideast	947	155,746
Great Lakes	511	31,041
Plains	170	14,654
Southeast	127	11,547
West/Far West	20	639
Total	**1,933**	**221,366**

Schools with Internet Access/E-Rate Program

In this survey, dioceses were asked to report on the number of schools which provide students with access to the Internet. The number of schools that make this technology available to students is listed in Exhibit 37. Since 1998, schools were able to apply for discounted telecommunications services under a program known as the E-Rate. The number of schools that received E-Rate discounts in the last school year as well as those that applied in 2017 is included in Exhibit 36. Not all dioceses provided this information. A listing by region and state is found in Appendix F.

EXHIBIT 37: Schools with Student Internet Access/E-Rate Program

	Schools with Internet Access		E-Rate Program	
	Internet Access		Received E-Rate	Applied for E-Rate
Region	Number	%	2015-2016	2016-2017
New England	378	96.7	173	181
Mideast	1,336	95.8	843	831
Great Lakes	1,365	88.0	572	787
Plains	658	81.8	359	349
Southeast	871	92.6	477	468
West/Far West	1,324	95.3	660	705
Total	**5,932**	**92.3**	**3,084**	**3,321**

DATABANK - REPORT A12

ACADEMIC YEAR: 2016-2017

Summary Report of Basic School Statistics

Schools and Enrollment: Sorted by Region

	Number of Schools			*Number of Students*		
Regional Totals	*Elementary/Middle*	*Secondary*	*Total*	*Elementary/Middle*	*Secondary*	*Total*
NEW ENGLAND	301	90	391	62,679	39,636	102,315
MIDEAST	1,107	290	1,397	283,156	147,897	431,053
GREAT LAKES	1,267	241	1,508	314,317	112,376	426,693
PLAINS	668	136	804	149,099	50,642	199,741
SOUTHEAST	744	197	941	220,557	92,378	312,935
WEST/FAR WEST	1,137	251	1,388	279,621	126,466	406,087
Total	**5,224**	**1,205**	**6,429**	**1,309,429**	**569,395**	**1,878,824**

DATABANK - REPORT A11
ACADEMIC YEAR: 2016-2017

Summary Report of Basic School Statistics

Schools and Enrollment

Sorted by Region, State, Diocese

STATE	NUMBER of SCHOOLS			NUMBER of STUDENTS		
ARCH/DIOCESE	ELEMENTARY/MIDDLE	SECONDARY	TOTAL	ELEMENTARY/MIDDLE	SECONDARY	TOTAL
CONNECTICUT	**89**	**22**	**111**	**16,807**	**10,031**	**26,838**
BRIDGEPORT	31	8	39	6,778	3,673	10,451
HARTFORD	44	9	53	8,306	4,312	12,618
NORWICH	14	5	19	1,723	2,046	3,769
MAINE	**11**	**2**	**13**	**2,036**	**617**	**2,653**
PORTLAND	11	2	13	2,036	617	2,653
MASSACHUSETTS	**138**	**49**	**187**	**32,002**	**21,798**	**53,800**
BOSTON	86	32	118	21,682	15,865	37,547
FALL RIVER	18	5	23	3,493	2,874	6,367
SPRINGFIELD	12	3	15	2,781	532	3,313
WORCESTER	22	9	31	4,046	2,527	6,573
NEW HAMPSHIRE	**21**	**6**	**27**	**3,469**	**2,148**	**5,617**
MANCHESTER	21	6	27	3,469	2,148	5,617
RHODE ISLAND	**32**	**7**	**39**	**6,921**	**4,507**	**11,428**
PROVIDENCE	32	7	39	6,921	4,507	11,428
VERMONT	**10**	**4**	**14**	**1,444**	**535**	**1,979**
BURLINGTON	10	4	14	1,444	535	1,979
NEW ENGLAND	**301**	**90**	**391**	**62,679**	**39,636**	**102,315**
DELAWARE	**27**	**9**	**36**	**6,299**	**3,793**	**10,092**
WILMINGTON	27	9	36	6,299	3,793	10,092
DISTRICT OF COLUMBIA	**75**	**20**	**95**	**16,607**	**10,249**	**26,856**
WASHINGTON	75	20	95	16,607	10,249	26,856
MARYLAND	**48**	**20**	**68**	**14,686**	**10,419**	**25,105**
BALTIMORE	48	20	68	14,686	10,419	25,105
NEW JERSEY	**181**	**60**	**241**	**47,888**	**28,690**	**76,578**
CAMDEN	28	9	37	7,783	4,630	12,413
METUCHEN	24	4	28	6,437	2,242	8,679
NEWARK	70	29	99	17,096	12,492	29,588
PATERSON	25	7	32	5,805	2,959	8,764
TRENTON	34	11	45	10,767	6,367	17,134

DATABANK - REPORT A11
ACADEMIC YEAR: 2016-2017

Summary Report of Basic School Statistics

Schools and Enrollment

Sorted by Region, State, Diocese

STATE	NUMBER of SCHOOLS			NUMBER of STUDENTS		
ARCH/DIOCESE	ELEMENTARY/MIDDLE	SECONDARY	TOTAL	ELEMENTARY/MIDDLE	SECONDARY	TOTAL
NEW YORK	**411**	**106**	**517**	**107,228**	**58,423**	**165,651**
ALBANY	19	7	26	4,171	2,088	6,259
BROOKLYN	86	18	104	26,287	11,977	38,264
BUFFALO	40	13	53	9,500	4,963	14,463
NEW YORK	170	46	216	43,681	23,323	67,004
OGDENSBURG	10	2	12	1,411	410	1,821
ROCHESTER	21	6	27	3,684	3,253	6,937
ROCKVILLE CENTRE	47	10	57	15,294	11,056	26,350
SYRACUSE	18	4	22	3,200	1,353	4,553
PENNSYLVANIA	**365**	**75**	**440**	**90,448**	**36,323**	**126,771**
ALLENTOWN	39	6	45	9,174	3,444	12,618
ALTOONA-JOHNSTOWN	18	4	22	3,037	1,058	4,095
ERIE	29	7	36	5,511	2,014	7,525
GREENSBURG	14	2	16	1,960	584	2,544
HARRISBURG	38	7	45	7,693	3,206	10,899
PHILADELPHIA	135	33	168	45,982	20,656	66,638
PITTSBURGH	76	12	88	13,557	4,051	17,608
SCRANTON	16	4	20	3,534	1,310	4,844
MIDEAST	**1,107**	**290**	**1,397**	**283,156**	**147,897**	**431,053**
ILLINOIS	**373**	**66**	**439**	**100,156**	**35,300**	**135,456**
BELLEVILLE	27	3	30	4,692	1,031	5,723
CHICAGO	183	34	217	54,962	21,133	76,095
JOLIET	47	7	54	14,620	4,770	19,390
PEORIA	37	7	44	8,610	2,386	10,996
ROCKFORD	39	8	47	8,582	3,747	12,329
SPRINGFIELD	40	7	47	8,690	2,233	10,923
INDIANA	**151**	**24**	**175**	**42,280**	**13,343**	**55,623**
EVANSVILLE	22	4	26	5,814	1,546	7,360
FT. WAYNE/S. BEND	39	4	43	10,647	3,280	13,927
GARY	17	3	20	4,695	1,327	6,023

DATABANK - REPORT A11
ACADEMIC YEAR: 2016-2017

Summary Report of Basic School Statistics

Schools and Enrollment

Sorted by Region, State, Diocese

STATE	NUMBER of SCHOOLS			NUMBER of STUDENTS		
ARCH/DIOCESE	**ELEMENTARY/MIDDLE**	**SECONDARY**	**TOTAL**	**ELEMENTARY/MIDDLE**	**SECONDARY**	**TOTAL**
INDIANAPOLIS	58	11	69	17,473	5,996	23,469
LAFAYETTE	15	2	17	3,650	1,194	4,844
MICHIGAN	**181**	**44**	**225**	**37,960**	**15,067**	**53,027**
DETROIT	69	24	93	19,436	9,788	29,224
GAYLORD	16	5	21	2,317	570	2,887
GRAND RAPIDS	25	5	30	5,098	1,452	6,550
KALAMAZOO	19	3	22	2,159	485	2,644
LANSING	30	4	34	6,063	2,318	8,381
MARQUETTE	9	0	9	1,167	0	1,167
SAGINAW	13	3	16	1,720	454	2,174
OHIO	**311**	**77**	**388**	**89,561**	**37,615**	**127,176**
CINCINNATI	89	23	112	29,139	12,696	41,835
CLEVELAND	90	20	110	30,450	12,709	43,159
COLUMBUS	42	11	53	11,431	4,661	16,092
STEUBENVILLE	10	3	13	1,554	358	1,912
TOLEDO	57	14	71	11,970	5,148	17,118
YOUNGSTOWN	23	6	29	5,017	2,043	7,060
WISCONSIN	**251**	**30**	**281**	**44,360**	**11,051**	**55,411**
GREEN BAY	49	6	55	7,089	2,075	9,164
LA CROSSE	53	7	60	5,440	1,279	6,719
MADISON	42	2	44	6,198	589	6,787
MILWAUKEE	92	15	107	23,664	7,108	30,772
SUPERIOR	15	0	15	1,969	0	1,969
GREAT LAKES	**1,267**	**241**	**1,508**	**314,317**	**112,376**	**426,693**
IOWA	**87**	**21**	**108**	**22,388**	**6,576**	**28,964**
DAVENPORT	13	5	18	3,648	1,269	4,917
DES MOINES	15	2	17	4,696	1,593	6,289
DUBUQUE	43	7	50	9,391	2,263	11,654
SIOUX CITY	16	7	23	4,653	1,451	6,104
KANSAS	**88**	**15**	**103**	**21,466**	**6,814**	**28,280**

DATABANK - REPORT A11
ACADEMIC YEAR: 2016-2017

Summary Report of Basic School Statistics

Schools and Enrollment

Sorted by Region, State, Diocese

STATE	NUMBER of SCHOOLS			NUMBER of STUDENTS		
ARCH/DIOCESE	ELEMENTARY/MIDDLE	SECONDARY	TOTAL	ELEMENTARY/MIDDLE	SECONDARY	TOTAL
DODGE CITY	6	0	6	802	0	802
KANSAS CITY	36	7	43	10,958	3,635	14,593
SALINA	11	4	15	1,707	651	2,358
WICHITA	35	4	39	7,999	2,528	10,527
MINNESOTA	**157**	**24**	**181**	**33,220**	**9,862**	**43,082**
CROOKSTON	8	1	9	1,249	150	1,399
DULUTH	10	0	10	1,452	0	1,452
NEW ULM	15	3	18	1,612	386	1,998
ST. CLOUD	28	2	30	4,129	919	5,048
ST. PAUL-MNPLS	80	14	94	21,463	7,408	28,871
WINONA	16	4	20	3,315	999	4,314
MISSOURI	**205**	**40**	**245**	**43,186**	**16,652**	**59,838**
JEFFERSON CITY	37	3	40	5,935	1,093	7,028
KANSAS CITY/ST. JOSEPH	33	7	40	7,005	3,245	10,250
SPRINGFIELD-CAPE GIR	23	3	26	3,319	1,021	4,340
ST. LOUIS	112	27	139	26,927	11,293	38,220
NEBRASKA	**86**	**28**	**114**	**20,855**	**8,364**	**29,219**
GRAND ISLAND	6	4	10	1,046	506	1,552
LINCOLN	26	6	32	5,452	2,384	7,836
OMAHA	54	18	72	14,357	5,474	19,831
NORTH DAKOTA	**24**	**4**	**28**	**3,762**	**1,051**	**4,813**
BISMARCK	11	3	14	1,979	721	2,700
FARGO	13	1	14	1,783	330	2,113
SOUTH DAKOTA	**21**	**4**	**25**	**4,222**	**1,323**	**5,545**
RAPID CITY	2	1	3	618	282	900
SIOUX FALLS	19	3	22	3,604	1,041	4,645
PLAINS	**668**	**136**	**804**	**149,099**	**50,642**	**199,741**
ALABAMA	**42**	**9**	**51**	**8,637**	**3,268**	**11,905**
BIRMINGHAM	22	6	28	4,485	1,689	6,174
MOBILE	20	3	23	4,152	1,579	5,731

DATABANK - REPORT A11
ACADEMIC YEAR: 2016-2017

Summary Report of Basic School Statistics

Schools and Enrollment

Sorted by Region, State, Diocese

STATE	NUMBER of SCHOOLS			NUMBER of STUDENTS		
ARCH/DIOCESE	ELEMENTARY/MIDDLE	SECONDARY	TOTAL	ELEMENTARY/MIDDLE	SECONDARY	TOTAL
ARKANSAS	**23**	**6**	**29**	**4,940**	**1,859**	**6,799**
LITTLE ROCK	23	6	29	4,940	1,859	6,799
FLORIDA	**183**	**41**	**224**	**59,740**	**24,814**	**84,554**
MIAMI	52	14	66	21,325	12,559	33,884
ORLANDO	37	5	42	11,344	3,165	14,509
PALM BEACH	14	3	17	4,716	1,386	6,102
PENSACOLA/TALAHASSEE	7	2	9	1,978	794	2,772
ST. AUGUSTINE	31	5	36	8,721	2,169	10,890
ST. PETERSBURG	29	8	37	8,614	3,255	11,869
VENICE	13	4	17	3,042	1,486	4,528
GEORGIA	**33**	**15**	**48**	**10,399**	**6,209**	**16,608**
ATLANTA	19	10	29	7,035	4,674	11,709
SAVANNAH	14	5	19	3,364	1,535	4,899
KENTUCKY	**96**	**23**	**119**	**25,851**	**10,573**	**36,424**
COVINGTON	28	9	37	6,728	3,035	9,763
LEXINGTON	14	2	16	2,638	944	3,582
LOUISVILLE	40	9	49	13,559	5,967	19,526
OWENSBORO	14	3	17	2,926	627	3,553
LOUISIANA	**140**	**51**	**191**	**51,951**	**24,994**	**76,945**
ALEXANDRIA	7	3	10	1,992	718	2,710
BATON ROUGE	25	9	34	11,017	3,873	14,890
HOUMA-THIBODAUX	10	3	13	3,467	1,872	5,339
LAFAYETTE	30	11	41	10,246	3,877	14,123
LAKE CHARLES	6	1	7	1,995	617	2,612
NEW ORLEANS	58	22	80	22,053	13,277	35,330
SHREVEPORT	4	2	6	1,181	760	1,941
MISSISSIPPI	**25**	**9**	**34**	**5,018**	**2,675**	**7,693**
BILOXI	10	5	15	2,352	1,604	3,956
JACKSON	15	4	19	2,666	1,071	3,737
NORTH CAROLINA	**43**	**5**	**48**	**12,899**	**3,462**	**16,361**
CHARLOTTE	16	3	19	5,323	1,883	7,206

DATABANK - REPORT A11
ACADEMIC YEAR: 2016-2017

Summary Report of Basic School Statistics

Schools and Enrollment

Sorted by Region, State, Diocese

STATE	NUMBER of SCHOOLS			NUMBER of STUDENTS		
ARCH/DIOCESE	ELEMENTARY/MIDDLE	SECONDARY	TOTAL	ELEMENTARY/MIDDLE	SECONDARY	TOTAL
RALEIGH	27	2	29	7,576	1,579	9,155
SOUTH CAROLINA	**28**	**7**	**35**	**5,091**	**2,182**	**7,273**
CHARLESTON	28	7	35	5,091	2,182	7,273
TENNESSEE	**43**	**11**	**54**	**11,123**	**5,261**	**16,384**
KNOXVILLE	8	2	10	2,173	1,039	3,212
MEMPHIS	19	6	25	4,968	2,483	7,451
NASHVILLE	16	3	19	3,982	1,739	5,721
VIRGINIA	**68**	**13**	**81**	**20,972**	**5,569**	**26,541**
ARLINGTON	43	5	48	13,631	3,912	17,543
RICHMOND	25	8	33	7,341	1,657	8,998
WEST VIRGINIA	**20**	**7**	**27**	**3,936**	**1,512**	**5,448**
WHEELING	20	7	27	3,936	1,512	5,448
SOUTHEAST	**744**	**197**	**941**	**220,557**	**92,378**	**312,935**
ALASKA	**6**	**3**	**9**	**692**	**266**	**958**
ANCHORAGE	4	2	6	340	142	482
FAIRBANKS	1	1	2	281	124	405
JUNEAU	1	0	1	71	0	71
ARIZONA	**47**	**12**	**59**	**13,377**	**7,227**	**20,604**
PHOENIX	28	6	34	8,709	4,994	13,703
TUCSON	19	6	25	4,668	2,233	6,901
CALIFORNIA	**542**	**116**	**658**	**139,180**	**68,745**	**207,925**
FRESNO	19	2	21	4,666	1,118	5,784
LOS ANGELES	216	51	267	52,719	25,875	78,594
MONTEREY	14	5	19	3,086	1,514	4,600
OAKLAND	45	9	54	11,117	5,710	16,827
ORANGE	34	7	41	12,020	6,559	18,579
SACRAMENTO	37	6	43	8,695	4,198	12,893
SAN BERNARDINO	27	3	30	6,008	1,491	7,499
SAN DIEGO	43	5	48	10,933	4,088	15,021
SAN FRANCISCO	58	14	72	16,442	8,124	24,566

DATABANK - REPORT A11
ACADEMIC YEAR: 2016-2017

Summary Report of Basic School Statistics

Schools and Enrollment

Sorted by Region, State, Diocese

STATE	NUMBER of SCHOOLS			NUMBER of STUDENTS		
ARCH/DIOCESE	ELEMENTARY/MIDDLE	SECONDARY	TOTAL	ELEMENTARY/MIDDLE	SECONDARY	TOTAL
SAN JOSE	27	6	33	8,573	7,043	15,616
SANTA ROSA	11	6	17	2,150	1,810	3,960
STOCKTON	11	2	13	2,771	1,215	3,986
COLORADO	**47**	**9**	**56**	**10,703**	**4,397**	**15,100**
COLORADO SPRINGS	7	1	8	1,306	253	1,559
DENVER	36	7	43	8,420	4,136	12,556
PUEBLO	4	1	5	977	8	985
HAWAII	**32**	**8**	**40**	**5,862**	**3,049**	**8,911**
HONOLULU	32	8	40	5,862	3,049	8,911
IDAHO	**14**	**2**	**16**	**2,469**	**821**	**3,290**
BOISE	14	2	16	2,469	821	3,290
MONTANA	**18**	**6**	**24**	**2,932**	**954**	**3,886**
GREAT FALLS/HELENA	18	6	24	2,932	954	3,886
NEVADA	**10**	**2**	**12**	**3,427**	**2,163**	**5,590**
LAS VEGAS	6	1	7	2,284	1,488	3,772
RENO	4	1	5	1,143	675	1,818
NEW MEXICO	**31**	**4**	**35**	**4,543**	**1,334**	**5,877**
GALLUP	11	1	12	1,131	100	1,231
LAS CRUCES	5	1	6	555	17	572
SANTA FE	15	2	17	2,857	1,217	4,074
OKLAHOMA	**30**	**4**	**34**	**7,051**	**2,528**	**9,579**
OKLAHOMA CITY	19	2	21	3,858	1,110	4,968
TULSA	11	2	13	3,193	1,418	4,611
OREGON	**44**	**10**	**54**	**9,448**	**5,753**	**15,201**
BAKER	4	0	4	452	0	452
PORTLAND	40	10	50	8,996	5,753	14,749
TEXAS	**214**	**56**	**270**	**54,846**	**20,121**	**74,967**
AMARILLO	4	1	5	613	72	685
AUSTIN	16	6	22	3,925	1,203	5,128
BEAUMONT	4	1	5	1,090	446	1,536

DATABANK - REPORT A11
ACADEMIC YEAR: 2016-2017

Summary Report of Basic School Statistics

Schools and Enrollment

Sorted by Region, State, Diocese

STATE	NUMBER of SCHOOLS			NUMBER of STUDENTS		
ARCH/DIOCESE	ELEMENTARY/MIDDLE	SECONDARY	TOTAL	ELEMENTARY/MIDDLE	SECONDARY	TOTAL
BROWNSVILLE	10	3	13	2,092	739	2,831
CORPUS CHRISTI	16	2	18	2,656	566	3,222
DALLAS	29	9	38	9,676	5,167	14,843
EL PASO	10	3	13	2,280	962	3,242
FORT WORTH	17	4	21	4,252	1,139	5,391
GALVESTON-HOUSTON	49	10	59	13,944	5,211	19,155
LAREDO	6	1	7	1,561	371	1,932
LUBBOCK	2	1	3	355	69	424
SAN ANGELO	3	0	3	838	0	838
SAN ANTONIO	32	10	42	8,558	3,379	11,937
TYLER	4	2	6	599	268	867
VICTORIA	12	3	15	2,407	529	2,936
UTAH	**13**	**3**	**16**	**3,620**	**1,611**	**5,231**
SALT LAKE CITY	13	3	16	3,620	1,611	5,231
WASHINGTON	**82**	**15**	**97**	**20,571**	**7,478**	**28,049**
SEATTLE	63	11	74	15,776	6,160	21,936
SPOKANE	13	3	16	3,196	1,100	4,296
YAKIMA	6	1	7	1,599	218	1,817
WYOMING	**7**	**1**	**8**	**900**	**19**	**919**
CHEYENNE	7	1	8	900	19	919
WEST/FAR WEST	**1,137**	**251**	**1,388**	**279,621**	**126,466**	**406,087**

Appendix C: Archdiocese/Diocese Ranked by Number of Students

NATIONAL CATHOLIC EDUCATIONAL ASSOCIATION

Archdiocese/Dioceses Ranked by Number of Students

DATABANK - REPORT D

ACADEMIC YEAR: 2016-2017

	ARCH/DIOCESE	STATE	SCHOOLS	STUDENTS
1	LOS ANGELES	CALIFORNIA	267	78,594
2	CHICAGO	ILLINOIS	217	76,095
3	NEW YORK	NEW YORK	216	67,004
4	PHILADELPHIA	PENNSYLVANIA	168	66,638
5	CLEVELAND	OHIO	110	43,159
6	CINCINNATI	OHIO	112	41,835
7	BROOKLYN	NEW YORK	104	38,264
8	ST. LOUIS	MISSOURI	139	38,220
9	BOSTON	MASSACHUSETTS	118	37,547
10	NEW ORLEANS	LOUISIANA	80	35,330
11	MIAMI	FLORIDA	66	33,884
12	MILWAUKEE	WISCONSIN	107	30,772
13	NEWARK	NEW JERSEY	99	29,588
14	DETROIT	MICHIGAN	93	29,224
15	ST. PAUL-MNPLS	MINNESOTA	94	28,871
16	WASHINGTON	DISTRICT OF COLUMBIA	95	26,856
17	ROCKVILLE CENTRE	NEW YORK	57	26,350
18	BALTIMORE	MARYLAND	68	25,105
19	SAN FRANCISCO	CALIFORNIA	72	24,566
20	INDIANAPOLIS	INDIANA	69	23,469
21	SEATTLE	WASHINGTON	74	21,936
22	OMAHA	NEBRASKA	72	19,831
23	LOUISVILLE	KENTUCKY	49	19,526
24	JOLIET	ILLINOIS	54	19,390
25	GALVESTON-HOUST	TEXAS	59	19,155
26	ORANGE	CALIFORNIA	41	18,579
27	PITTSBURGH	PENNSYLVANIA	88	17,608
28	ARLINGTON	VIRGINIA	48	17,543
29	TRENTON	NEW JERSEY	45	17,134
30	TOLEDO	OHIO	71	17,118
31	OAKLAND	CALIFORNIA	54	16,827
32	COLUMBUS	OHIO	53	16,092
33	SAN JOSE	CALIFORNIA	33	15,616
34	SAN DIEGO	CALIFORNIA	48	15,021
35	BATON ROUGE	LOUISIANA	34	14,890
36	DALLAS	TEXAS	38	14,843
37	PORTLAND	OREGON	50	14,749
38	KANSAS CITY	KANSAS	43	14,593
39	ORLANDO	FLORIDA	42	14,509
40	BUFFALO	NEW YORK	53	14,463
41	LAFAYETTE	LOUISIANA	41	14,123
42	FT. WAYNE/S. BEND	INDIANA	43	13,927
43	PHOENIX	ARIZONA	34	13,703
44	SACRAMENTO	CALIFORNIA	43	12,893
45	HARTFORD	CONNECTICUT	53	12,618
46	ALLENTOWN	PENNSYLVANIA	45	12,618
47	DENVER	COLORADO	43	12,556
48	CAMDEN	NEW JERSEY	37	12,413
49	ROCKFORD	ILLINOIS	47	12,329
50	SAN ANTONIO	TEXAS	42	11,937
51	ST. PETERSBURG	FLORIDA	37	11,869
52	ATLANTA	GEORGIA	29	11,709

Appendix C: Archdiocese/Diocese Ranked by Number of Students

NATIONAL CATHOLIC EDUCATIONAL ASSOCIATION

Archdiocese/Dioceses Ranked by Number of Students

DATABANK - REPORT D

ACADEMIC YEAR: 2016-2017

	ARCH/DIOCESE	STATE	SCHOOLS	STUDENTS
53	DUBUQUE	IOWA	50	11,654
54	PROVIDENCE	RHODE ISLAND	39	11,428
55	PEORIA	ILLINOIS	44	10,996
56	SPRINGFIELD	ILLINOIS	47	10,923
57	HARRISBURG	PENNSYLVANIA	45	10,899
58	ST. AUGUSTINE	FLORIDA	36	10,890
59	WICHITA	KANSAS	39	10,527
60	BRIDGEPORT	CONNECTICUT	39	10,451
61	KANSAS CITY/ST. JO	MISSOURI	40	10,250
62	WILMINGTON	DELAWARE	36	10,092
63	COVINGTON	KENTUCKY	37	9,763
64	GREEN BAY	WISCONSIN	55	9,164
65	RALEIGH	NORTH CAROLINA	29	9,155
66	RICHMOND	VIRGINIA	33	8,998
67	HONOLULU	HAWAII	40	8,911
68	PATERSON	NEW JERSEY	32	8,764
69	METUCHEN	NEW JERSEY	28	8,679
70	LANSING	MICHIGAN	34	8,381
71	LINCOLN	NEBRASKA	32	7,836
72	ERIE	PENNSYLVANIA	36	7,525
73	SAN BERNARDINO	CALIFORNIA	30	7,499
74	MEMPHIS	TENNESSEE	25	7,451
75	EVANSVILLE	INDIANA	26	7,360
76	CHARLESTON	SOUTH CAROLINA	35	7,273
77	CHARLOTTE	NORTH CAROLINA	19	7,206
78	YOUNGSTOWN	OHIO	29	7,060
79	JEFFERSON CITY	MISSOURI	40	7,028
80	ROCHESTER	NEW YORK	27	6,937
81	TUCSON	ARIZONA	25	6,901
82	LITTLE ROCK	ARKANSAS	29	6,799
83	MADISON	WISCONSIN	44	6,787
84	LA CROSSE	WISCONSIN	60	6,719
85	WORCESTER	MASSACHUSETTS	31	6,573
86	GRAND RAPIDS	MICHIGAN	30	6,550
87	FALL RIVER	MASSACHUSETTS	23	6,367
88	DES MOINES	IOWA	17	6,289
89	ALBANY	NEW YORK	26	6,259
90	BIRMINGHAM	ALABAMA	28	6,174
91	SIOUX CITY	IOWA	23	6,104
92	PALM BEACH	FLORIDA	17	6,102
93	GARY	INDIANA	20	6,023
94	FRESNO	CALIFORNIA	21	5,784
95	MOBILE	ALABAMA	23	5,731
96	BELLEVILLE	ILLINOIS	30	5,723
97	NASHVILLE	TENNESSEE	19	5,721
98	MANCHESTER	NEW HAMPSHIRE	27	5,617
99	WHEELING	WEST VIRGINIA	27	5,448
100	FORT WORTH	TEXAS	21	5,391
101	HOUMA-THIBODAUX	LOUISIANA	13	5,339
102	SALT LAKE CITY	UTAH	16	5,231
103	AUSTIN	TEXAS	22	5,128
104	ST. CLOUD	MINNESOTA	30	5,048

Appendix C: Archdiocese/Diocese Ranked by Number of Students

NATIONAL CATHOLIC EDUCATIONAL ASSOCIATION

Archdiocese/Dioceses Ranked by Number of Students

DATABANK - REPORT D
ACADEMIC YEAR: 2016-2017

	ARCH/DIOCESE	STATE	SCHOOLS	STUDENTS
105	OKLAHOMA CITY	OKLAHOMA	21	4,968
106	DAVENPORT	IOWA	18	4,917
107	SAVANNAH	GEORGIA	19	4,899
108	SCRANTON	PENNSYLVANIA	20	4,844
109	LAFAYETTE	INDIANA	17	4,844
110	SIOUX FALLS	SOUTH DAKOTA	22	4,645
111	TULSA	OKLAHOMA	13	4,611
112	MONTEREY	CALIFORNIA	19	4,600
113	SYRACUSE	NEW YORK	22	4,553
114	VENICE	FLORIDA	17	4,528
115	SPRINGFIELD-CAPE	MISSOURI	26	4,340
116	WINONA	MINNESOTA	20	4,314
117	SPOKANE	WASHINGTON	16	4,296
118	ALTOONA-JOHNSTO	PENNSYLVANIA	22	4,095
119	SANTA FE	NEW MEXICO	17	4,074
120	STOCKTON	CALIFORNIA	13	3,986
121	SANTA ROSA	CALIFORNIA	17	3,960
122	BILOXI	MISSISSIPPI	15	3,956
123	GREAT FALLS/HELE	MONTANA	24	3,886
124	LAS VEGAS	NEVADA	7	3,772
125	NORWICH	CONNECTICUT	19	3,769
126	JACKSON	MISSISSIPPI	19	3,737
127	LEXINGTON	KENTUCKY	16	3,582
128	OWENSBORO	KENTUCKY	17	3,553
129	SPRINGFIELD	MASSACHUSETTS	15	3,313
130	BOISE	IDAHO	16	3,290
131	EL PASO	TEXAS	13	3,242
132	CORPUS CHRISTI	TEXAS	18	3,222
133	KNOXVILLE	TENNESSEE	10	3,212
134	VICTORIA	TEXAS	15	2,936
135	GAYLORD	MICHIGAN	21	2,887
136	BROWNSVILLE	TEXAS	13	2,831
137	PENSACOLA/TALAH	FLORIDA	9	2,772
138	ALEXANDRIA	LOUISIANA	10	2,710
139	BISMARCK	NORTH DAKOTA	14	2,700
140	PORTLAND	MAINE	13	2,653
141	KALAMAZOO	MICHIGAN	22	2,644
142	LAKE CHARLES	LOUISIANA	7	2,612
143	GREENSBURG	PENNSYLVANIA	16	2,544
144	SALINA	KANSAS	15	2,358
145	SAGINAW	MICHIGAN	16	2,174
146	FARGO	NORTH DAKOTA	14	2,113
147	NEW ULM	MINNESOTA	18	1,998
148	BURLINGTON	VERMONT	14	1,979
149	SUPERIOR	WISCONSIN	15	1,969
150	SHREVEPORT	LOUISIANA	6	1,941
151	LAREDO	TEXAS	7	1,932
152	STEUBENVILLE	OHIO	13	1,912
153	OGDENSBURG	NEW YORK	12	1,821
154	RENO	NEVADA	5	1,818
155	YAKIMA	WASHINGTON	7	1,817
156	COLORADO SPRING	COLORADO	8	1,559

Appendix C: Archdiocese/Diocese Ranked by Number of Students

NATIONAL CATHOLIC EDUCATIONAL ASSOCIATION

Archdiocese/Dioceses Ranked by Number of Students

DATABANK - REPORT D
ACADEMIC YEAR: 2016-2017

	ARCH/DIOCESE	STATE	SCHOOLS	STUDENTS
157	GRAND ISLAND	NEBRASKA	10	1,552
158	BEAUMONT	TEXAS	5	1,536
159	DULUTH	MINNESOTA	10	1,452
160	CROOKSTON	MINNESOTA	9	1,399
161	GALLUP	NEW MEXICO	12	1,231
162	MARQUETTE	MICHIGAN	9	1,167
163	PUEBLO	COLORADO	5	985
164	CHEYENNE	WYOMING	8	919
165	RAPID CITY	SOUTH DAKOTA	3	900
166	TYLER	TEXAS	6	867
167	SAN ANGELO	TEXAS	3	838
168	DODGE CITY	KANSAS	6	802
169	AMARILLO	TEXAS	5	685
170	LAS CRUCES	NEW MEXICO	6	572
171	ANCHORAGE	ALASKA	6	482
172	BAKER	OREGON	4	452
173	LUBBOCK	TEXAS	3	424
174	FAIRBANKS	ALASKA	2	405
175	JUNEAU	ALASKA	1	71
		Grand Total:	**6,429**	**1,878,824**

Appendix D: States Ranked by Number of Students

NATIONAL CATHOLIC EDUCATIONAL ASSOCIATION

States Ranked by Number of Students

DATABANK - REPORT E

ACADEMIC YEAR: 2016-2017

	STATE	STUDENTS	SCHOOLS
1	CALIFORNIA	207,925	658
2	NEW YORK	165,651	517
3	ILLINOIS	135,456	439
4	OHIO	127,176	388
5	PENNSYLVANIA	126,771	440
6	FLORIDA	84,554	224
7	LOUISIANA	76,945	191
8	NEW JERSEY	76,578	241
9	TEXAS	74,967	270
10	MISSOURI	59,838	245
11	INDIANA	55,623	175
12	WISCONSIN	55,411	281
13	MASSACHUSETTS	53,800	187
14	MICHIGAN	53,027	225
15	MINNESOTA	43,082	181
16	KENTUCKY	36,424	119
17	NEBRASKA	29,219	114
18	IOWA	28,964	108
19	KANSAS	28,280	103
20	WASHINGTON	28,049	97
21	DISTRICT OF COLUMBIA	26,856	95
22	CONNECTICUT	26,838	111
23	VIRGINIA	26,541	81
24	MARYLAND	25,105	68
25	ARIZONA	20,604	59
26	GEORGIA	16,608	48
27	TENNESSEE	16,384	54
28	NORTH CAROLINA	16,361	48
29	OREGON	15,201	54
30	COLORADO	15,100	56
31	ALABAMA	11,905	51
32	RHODE ISLAND	11,428	39
33	DELAWARE	10,092	36
34	OKLAHOMA	9,579	34
35	HAWAII	8,911	40
36	MISSISSIPPI	7,693	34
37	SOUTH CAROLINA	7,273	35
38	ARKANSAS	6,799	29
39	NEW MEXICO	5,877	35
40	NEW HAMPSHIRE	5,617	27
41	NEVADA	5,590	12
42	SOUTH DAKOTA	5,545	25
43	WEST VIRGINIA	5,448	27
44	UTAH	5,231	16
45	NORTH DAKOTA	4,813	28
46	MONTANA	3,886	24
47	IDAHO	3,290	16
48	MAINE	2,653	13
49	VERMONT	1,979	14
50	ALASKA	958	9
51	WYOMING	919	8
	GRAND TOTAL	**1,878,824**	**6,429**

Appendix E: Summary Report School Locations

DATABANK - REPORT I2b
ACADEMIC YEAR: 2016-2017

Summary Report: School Location - Sorted by Region

	ELEMENTARY/MIDDLE					SECONDARY					NATIONAL
REGION	**Urban**	**Inner City**	**Suburban**	**Rural**	**Total**	**Urban**	**Inner City**	**Suburban**	**Rural**	**Total**	**Total**
NEW ENGLAND	77	63	132	29	301	27	16	37	10	90	391
	5.0%	12.4%	6.4%	2.6%	5.8%	6.2%	13.4%	7.9%	5.6%	7.5%	6.1%
MIDEAST	258	145	578	126	1107	81	38	148	23	290	1,397
	16.9%	28.5%	28.1%	11.1%	21.2%	18.5%	31.9%	31.6%	12.8%	24.1%	21.7%
GREAT LAKES	355	71	479	362	1267	97	15	90	39	241	1,508
	23.3%	14.0%	23.3%	31.9%	24.3%	22.1%	12.6%	19.2%	21.8%	20.0%	23.5%
PLAINS	147	24	165	332	668	39	5	37	55	136	804
	9.6%	4.7%	8.0%	29.2%	12.8%	8.9%	4.2%	7.9%	30.7%	11.3%	12.5%
SOUTHEAST	223	54	327	140	744	67	12	85	33	197	941
	14.6%	10.6%	15.9%	12.3%	14.2%	15.3%	10.1%	18.2%	18.4%	16.3%	14.6%
WEST/FAR WEST	466	151	373	147	1137	128	33	71	19	251	1,388
	30.5%	29.7%	18.2%	12.9%	21.8%	29.2%	27.7%	15.2%	10.6%	20.8%	21.6%
GRAND TOTALS	1526	508	2054	1136	5224	439	119	468	179	1205	6,429
	29.2%	9.7%	39.3%	21.7%		36.4%	9.9%	38.8%	14.9%		

	All Schools		**Elementary - Middle**		**Secondary**	
Urban:	1,965	30.6%	1,526	29.2%	439	36.4%
Inner City:	627	9.8%	508	9.7%	119	9.9%
Suburban:	2,522	39.2%	2,054	39.3%	468	38.8%
Rural:	1,315	20.5%	1,136	21.7%	179	14.9%
	6,429		5,224		1,205	

DATABANK - REPORT J
ACADEMIC YEAR: 2016-2017

NATIONAL CATHOLIC EDUCATIONAL ASSOCIATION (NCEA)
Government Funded Programs
by Region, State and Diocese

	Title I Services Received		Nutrition Programs	Students Receive		Transportation		E-rate 2016	E-rate 2017
	Schools	Students	Schools	Breakfast	Lunch	Schools	Students	Schools Received	Schools Applied
NEW ENGLAND									
CONNECTICUT	**63**	**1,250**	**30**	**780**	**987**	**80**	**3,259**	**43**	**44**
BRIDGEPORT	11	660	10	668	718	22	2,204	26	29
HARTFORD	43	450	14	100	208	51	505	5	5
NORWICH	9	140	6	12	61	7	550	12	10
MAINE	**10**	**121**	**6**	**42**	**94**	**4**	**74**	**8**	**10**
PORTLAND	10	121	6	42	94	4	74	8	10
MASSACHUSETTS	**77**	**2,886**	**74**	**5,461**	**6,730**	**58**	**3,550**	**84**	**89**
BOSTON	44	2,195	45	3,230	4,104	36	1,711	52	55
FALL RIVER	9	164	6	591	625	6	352	6	6
SPRINGFIELD	10	244	13	1,490	1,679	8	1,079	4	6
WORCESTER	14	283	10	150	322	8	408	22	22
NEW HAMPSHIRE	**9**	**129**	**4**	**0**	**30**	**4**	**48**	**3**	**4**
MANCHESTER	9	129	4	0	30	4	48	3	4
RHODE ISLAND	**27**	**577**	**8**	**424**	**486**	**11**	**807**	**26**	**26**
PROVIDENCE	27	577	8	424	486	11	807	26	26
VERMONT	**5**	**90**	**10**	**89**	**195**	**1**	**1**	**9**	**8**
BURLINGTON	5	90	10	89	195	1	1	9	8
NEW ENGLAND	**191**	**5,053**	**132**	**6,796**	**8,522**	**158**	**7,739**	**173**	**181**
MIDEAST									
DELAWARE	**18**	**170**	**3**	**176**	**176**	**13**	**2,435**	**20**	**21**
WILMINGTON	18	170	3	176	176	13	2,435	20	21
DISTRICT OF COLUMBIA	**34**	**538**	**9**	**400**	**799**	**10**	**563**	**37**	**34**
WASHINGTON	34	538	9	400	799	10	563	37	34
MARYLAND	**26**	**388**	**14**	**1,102**	**1,116**	**4**	**153**	**67**	**66**
BALTIMORE	26	388	14	1,102	1,116	4	153	67	66
NEW JERSEY	**86**	**2,944**	**45**	**3,632**	**4,376**	**204**	**30,952**	**135**	**119**
CAMDEN	18	790	8	789	999	36	7,269	31	19

DATABANK - REPORT J
ACADEMIC YEAR: 2016-2017

NATIONAL CATHOLIC EDUCATIONAL ASSOCIATION (NCEA)
Government Funded Programs
by Region, State and Diocese

	Title I Services Received		Nutrition Programs	Students Receive		Transportation		E-rate 2016	E-rate 2017
	Schools	Students	Schools	Breakfast	Lunch	Schools	Students	Schools Received	Schools Applied
METUCHEN	5	56	3	0	108	23	4,562	12	9
NEWARK	42	1,405	18	1,947	2,428	80	8,333	48	50
PATERSON	10	291	7	399	286	27	2,925	21	16
TRENTON	11	402	9	497	555	38	7,863	23	25
NEW YORK	**284**	**15,091**	**190**	**19,847**	**22,412**	**395**	**70,785**	**383**	**385**
ALBANY	23	0	11	423	563	26	4,698	28	28
BROOKLYN	69	5,166	42	3,999	4,269	95	14,528	92	95
BUFFALO	39	1,438	38	1,148	1,887	53	9,725	40	42
NEW YORK	88	6,160	55	13,594	14,418	128	17,327	122	124
OGDENSBURG	12	445	9	65	236	10	752	11	11
ROCHESTER	23	908	10	251	398	10	2,404	21	18
ROCKVILLE CENTRE	14	532	3	47	3	57	19,869	49	49
SYRACUSE	16	442	22	320	638	16	1,482	20	18
PENNSYLVANIA	**298**	**14,784**	**206**	**14,279**	**18,605**	**321**	**50,858**	**201**	**206**
ALLENTOWN	35	1,219	11	382	958	45	7,791	34	34
ALTOONA-JOHNSTOWN	19	322	20	393	649	19	2,223	13	14
ERIE	24	552	18	341	850	14	2,650	25	26
GREENSBURG	13	229	8	118	314	15	0	13	13
HARRISBURG	37	973	18	306	1,073	27	4,236	30	32
PHILADELPHIA	107	10,059	72	11,532	12,435	100	17,789	51	56
PITTSBURGH	48	1,215	49	1,080	1,903	88	14,837	35	31
SCRANTON	15	215	10	127	423	13	1,332	0	0
MIDEAST	**746**	**33,915**	**467**	**39,436**	**47,484**	**947**	**155,746**	**843**	**831**
GREAT LAKES									
ILLINOIS	**218**	**7,423**	**230**	**7,859**	**14,400**	**30**	**1,623**	**92**	**286**
BELLEVILLE	22	470	27	115	416	6	184	10	8
CHICAGO	111	5,170	123	7,332	12,390	0	0	0	192
JOLIET	11	215	0	64	343	10	685	20	19
PEORIA	21	412	31	115	95	3	106	25	28
ROCKFORD	21	585	13	107	359	6	475	13	14
SPRINGFIELD	32	571	36	126	797	5	173	24	25
INDIANA	**123**	**4,169**	**150**	**5,836**	**11,346**	**20**	**842**	**71**	**76**

DATABANK - REPORT J
ACADEMIC YEAR: 2016-2017

NATIONAL CATHOLIC EDUCATIONAL ASSOCIATION (NCEA)
Government Funded Programs
by Region, State and Diocese

	Title I Services Received		Nutrition Programs Students Receive			Transportation		E-rate 2016	E-rate 2017
	Schools	Students	Schools	Breakfast	Lunch	Schools	Students	Schools Received	Schools Applied
EVANSVILLE	12	199	26	397	1,097	5	325	3	4
FT. WAYNE/S. BEND	32	1,152	38	1,127	3,512	5	138	14	14
GARY	15	503	15	970	1,580	0	199	20	20
INDIANAPOLIS	51	2,045	57	3,172	4,555	6	72	27	30
LAFAYETTE	13	270	14	170	602	4	108	7	8
MICHIGAN	**143**	**2,293**	**163**	**1,792**	**3,588**	**83**	**2,589**	**74**	**74**
DETROIT	63	775	87	1,082	1,373	30	952	28	34
GAYLORD	14	138	14	18	269	9	171	11	11
GRAND RAPIDS	18	573	23	348	835	15	656	0	0
KALAMAZOO	12	135	12	11	155	10	251	14	9
LANSING	19	411	23	52	483	5	473	15	14
MARQUETTE	9	149	4	160	219	6	63	4	4
SAGINAW	8	112	0	121	254	8	23	2	2
OHIO	**285**	**8,755**	**293**	**7,726**	**21,366**	**162**	**15,167**	**208**	**208**
CINCINNATI	86	3,253	78	0	6,075	0	0	0	0
CLEVELAND	84	2,211	85	3,982	7,771	60	5,305	84	84
COLUMBUS	32	892	41	1,454	2,670	40	4,588	40	40
STEUBENVILLE	8	109	1	31	116	5	259	9	8
TOLEDO	53	1,405	65	1,142	2,989	32	2,471	54	54
YOUNGSTOWN	22	885	23	1,117	1,745	25	2,544	21	22
WISCONSIN	**186**	**4,481**	**199**	**8,910**	**12,260**	**216**	**10,820**	**127**	**143**
GREEN BAY	43	148	45	208	817	47	2,646	19	25
LA CROSSE	36	209	56	157	830	60	855	21	27
MADISON	34	294	29	112	326	39	2,300	16	17
MILWAUKEE	61	3,727	59	8,360	10,001	56	4,350	66	65
SUPERIOR	12	103	10	73	286	14	669	5	9
GREAT LAKES	**955**	**27,121**	**1,035**	**32,123**	**62,960**	**511**	**31,041**	**572**	**787**
PLAINS									
IOWA	**69**	**950**	**105**	**2,438**	**4,644**	**80**	**8,749**	**80**	**75**
DAVENPORT	8	215	14	303	602	10	843	12	12
DES MOINES	11	174	17	718	977	8	1,342	6	5
DUBUQUE	32	270	50	749	1,785	43	4,419	42	38

DATABANK - REPORT J
ACADEMIC YEAR: 2016-2017

NATIONAL CATHOLIC EDUCATIONAL ASSOCIATION (NCEA)
Government Funded Programs
by Region, State and Diocese

	Title I Services Received		Nutrition Programs	Students Receive		Transportation		E-rate 2016	E-rate 2017
	Schools	Students	Schools	Breakfast	Lunch	Schools	Students	Schools Received	Schools Applied
SIOUX CITY	18	291	24	668	1,280	19	2,145	20	20
KANSAS	**67**	**1,601**	**90**	**1,113**	**5,086**	**24**	**254**	**53**	**53**
DODGE CITY	5	130	6	18	154	1	8	2	2
KANSAS CITY	21	607	34	887	1,924	8	138	14	14
SALINA	15	153	15	208	433	15	108	15	15
WICHITA	26	711	35	0	2,575	0	0	22	22
MINNESOTA	**71**	**1,024**	**77**	**705**	**5,744**	**52**	**5,034**	**26**	**28**
CROOKSTON	9	106	9	259	327	9	912	5	5
DULUTH	6	72	5	22	68	5	232	1	0
NEW ULM	15	157	18	184	285	18	1,143	9	10
ST. CLOUD	25	409	26	76	645	9	978	5	5
ST. PAUL-MNPLS	0	0	0	0	3,810	0	0	0	0
WINONA	16	280	19	164	609	11	1,769	6	8
MISSOURI	**122**	**1,344**	**152**	**1,397**	**13,860**	**1**	**240**	**95**	**96**
JEFFERSON CITY	25	190	35	75	675	0	0	28	30
KANSAS CITY/ST. JOSEPH	13	251	20	615	973	1	240	13	15
SPRINGFIELD-CAPE GIR	26	129	26	217	437	0	0	4	3
ST. LOUIS	58	774	71	490	11,775	0	0	50	48
NEBRASKA	**63**	**1,076**	**97**	**1,598**	**4,350**	**7**	**252**	**84**	**77**
GRAND ISLAND	5	39	7	0	175	2	9	4	4
LINCOLN	16	302	32	469	1,678	2	118	31	30
OMAHA	42	735	58	1,129	2,497	3	125	49	43
NORTH DAKOTA	**20**	**158**	**28**	**316**	**477**	**5**	**124**	**10**	**9**
BISMARCK	9	62	14	127	215	2	64	4	3
FARGO	11	96	14	189	262	3	60	6	6
SOUTH DAKOTA	**13**	**125**	**22**	**88**	**483**	**1**	**1**	**11**	**11**
RAPID CITY	3	26	3	50	50	0	0	0	0
SIOUX FALLS	10	99	19	38	433	1	1	11	11
PLAINS	**425**	**6,278**	**571**	**7,655**	**34,644**	**170**	**14,654**	**359**	**349**

SOUTHEAST

DATABANK - REPORT J
ACADEMIC YEAR: 2016-2017

NATIONAL CATHOLIC EDUCATIONAL ASSOCIATION (NCEA)
Government Funded Programs
by Region, State and Diocese

	Title I Services Received		Nutrition Programs	Students Receive		Transportation		E-rate 2016	E-rate 2017
	Schools	Students	Schools	Breakfast	Lunch	Schools	Students	Schools Received	Schools Applied
ALABAMA	**15**	**920**	**11**	**165**	**923**	**1**	**1**	**9**	**6**
BIRMINGHAM	7	654	5	0	480	0	0	3	4
MOBILE	8	266	6	165	443	1	1	6	2
ARKANSAS	**15**	**428**	**13**	**46**	**514**	**1**	**9**	**6**	**7**
LITTLE ROCK	15	428	13	46	514	1	9	6	7
FLORIDA	**142**	**5,927**	**28**	**4,177**	**3,896**	**5**	**200**	**135**	**134**
MIAMI	40	2,599	14	2,376	1,859	2	46	31	34
ORLANDO	29	957	6	833	838	1	1	37	35
PALM BEACH	12	427	1	145	145	1	145	8	9
PENSACOLA/TALAHASSEE	7	219	1	0	94	1	8	4	4
ST. AUGUSTINE	13	348	2	412	411	0	0	23	25
ST. PETERSBURG	29	1,101	4	411	467	0	0	18	16
VENICE	12	276	0	0	82	0	0	14	11
GEORGIA	**15**	**209**	**4**	**108**	**200**	**0**	**0**	**21**	**21**
ATLANTA	11	116	1	0	30	0	0	20	20
SAVANNAH	4	93	3	108	170	0	0	1	1
KENTUCKY	**59**	**1,436**	**87**	**1,254**	**2,500**	**34**	**3,973**	**49**	**55**
COVINGTON	21	451	31	288	844	11	1,692	13	13
LEXINGTON	13	181	9	122	256	0	0	7	6
LOUISVILLE	13	358	31	332	931	14	1,709	20	26
OWENSBORO	12	446	16	512	469	9	572	9	10
LOUISIANA	**120**	**5,242**	**146**	**8,817**	**12,199**	**72**	**6,739**	**111**	**103**
ALEXANDRIA	6	331	9	520	819	5	121	6	6
BATON ROUGE	16	838	22	2,050	2,129	11	2,732	23	23
HOUMA-THIBODAUX	10	194	12	369	500	8	619	9	7
LAFAYETTE	23	825	30	256	1,220	18	1,147	17	18
LAKE CHARLES	6	117	7	0	195	3	101	7	7
NEW ORLEANS	56	2,889	62	5,399	7,070	27	2,019	49	42
SHREVEPORT	3	48	4	223	266	0	0	0	0
MISSISSIPPI	**22**	**852**	**14**	**602**	**751**	**1**	**1**	**26**	**26**

NATIONAL CATHOLIC EDUCATIONAL ASSOCIATION (NCEA)
Government Funded Programs
by Region, State and Diocese

	Title I Services Received		Nutrition Programs	Students Receive		Transportation		E-rate 2016	E-rate 2017
	Schools	Students	Schools	Breakfast	Lunch	Schools	Students	Schools Received	Schools Applied
BILOXI	9	440	9	234	332	0	0	10	10
JACKSON	13	412	5	368	419	1	1	16	16
NORTH CAROLINA	**15**	**271**	**4**	**0**	**56**	**1**	**5**	**40**	**41**
CHARLOTTE	8	123	0	0	0	1	5	19	19
RALEIGH	7	148	4	0	56	0	0	21	22
SOUTH CAROLINA	**3**	**75**	**2**	**136**	**131**	**0**	**0**	**20**	**22**
CHARLESTON	3	75	2	136	131	0	0	20	22
TENNESSEE	**17**	**1,127**	**14**	**1,577**	**1,782**	**2**	**10**	**19**	**22**
KNOXVILLE	6	285	4	0	116	0	0	2	3
MEMPHIS	11	667	10	1,577	1,604	1	4	9	11
NASHVILLE	0	175	0	0	62	1	6	8	8
VIRGINIA	**26**	**492**	**6**	**0**	**121**	**1**	**1**	**25**	**20**
ARLINGTON	14	278	3	0	30	1	1	7	6
RICHMOND	12	214	3	0	91	0	0	18	14
WEST VIRGINIA	**15**	**315**	**14**	**116**	**325**	**9**	**608**	**16**	**11**
WHEELING	15	315	14	116	325	9	608	16	11
SOUTHEAST	**464**	**17,294**	**343**	**16,998**	**23,398**	**127**	**11,547**	**477**	**468**
WEST/FAR WEST									
ALASKA	**0**	**0**	**0**	**0**	**0**	**0**	**0**	**0**	**1**
ANCHORAGE	0	0	0	0	0	0	0	0	1
FAIRBANKS	0	0	0	0	0	0	0	0	0
JUNEAU	0	0	0	0	0	0	0	0	0
ARIZONA	**41**	**1,744**	**27**	**3,357**	**4,364**	**0**	**0**	**38**	**38**
PHOENIX	24	589	15	2,076	2,532	0	0	27	27
TUCSON	17	1,155	12	1,281	1,832	0	0	11	11
CALIFORNIA	**292**	**12,442**	**189**	**9,401**	**17,106**	**4**	**253**	**338**	**348**
FRESNO	9	261	2	38	38	0	0	9	9
LOS ANGELES	138	7,287	151	7,641	13,694	0	0	196	188
MONTEREY	1	175	0	0	0	0	0	6	9

DATABANK - REPORT J
ACADEMIC YEAR: 2016-2017

NATIONAL CATHOLIC EDUCATIONAL ASSOCIATION (NCEA)
Government Funded Programs
by Region, State and Diocese

	Title I Services Received		Nutrition Programs	Students Receive		Transportation		E-rate 2016	E-rate 2017
	Schools	Students	Schools	Breakfast	Lunch	Schools	Students	Schools Received	Schools Applied
OAKLAND	24	1,223	2	601	612	1	2	34	44
ORANGE	33	521	1	113	481	0	0	35	36
SACRAMENTO	26	531	4	337	495	1	10	13	13
SAN BERNARDINO	11	676	1	0	18	0	0	30	30
SAN DIEGO	21	496	5	0	209	1	55	8	11
SAN FRANCISCO	20	911	16	361	1,126	0	0	0	0
SAN JOSE	1	58	2	217	217	1	186	1	2
SANTA ROSA	3	131	2	49	49	0	0	3	4
STOCKTON	5	172	3	44	167	0	0	3	2
COLORADO	**18**	**498**	**20**	**864**	**1,443**	**1**	**25**	**16**	**17**
COLORADO SPRINGS	2	40	2	0	95	0	0	5	5
DENVER	14	406	16	850	1,310	1	25	9	10
PUEBLO	2	52	2	14	38	0	0	2	2
HAWAII	**18**	**477**	**7**	**101**	**97**	**0**	**0**	**10**	**13**
HONOLULU	18	477	7	101	97	0	0	10	13
IDAHO	**9**	**179**	**10**	**82**	**255**	**0**	**0**	**5**	**6**
BOISE	9	179	10	82	255	0	0	5	6
MONTANA	**20**	**621**	**21**	**890**	**1,199**	**0**	**0**	**23**	**23**
GREAT FALLS/HELENA	20	621	21	890	1,199	0	0	23	23
NEVADA	**6**	**106**	**0**	**0**	**0**	**0**	**0**	**1**	**1**
LAS VEGAS	2	31	0	0	0	0	0	0	0
RENO	4	75	0	0	0	0	0	1	1
NEW MEXICO	**22**	**518**	**20**	**701**	**1,149**	**0**	**0**	**18**	**19**
GALLUP	7	188	9	599	626	0	0	10	10
LAS CRUCES	4	71	1	0	42	0	0	0	0
SANTA FE	11	259	10	102	481	0	0	8	9
OKLAHOMA	**16**	**596**	**15**	**560**	**923**	**0**	**0**	**15**	**14**
OKLAHOMA CITY	10	350	12	322	653	0	0	6	6
TULSA	6	246	3	238	270	0	0	9	8
OREGON	**26**	**492**	**14**	**673**	**724**	**2**	**117**	**13**	**12**

DATABANK - REPORT J
ACADEMIC YEAR: 2016-2017

NATIONAL CATHOLIC EDUCATIONAL ASSOCIATION (NCEA)
Government Funded Programs
by Region, State and Diocese

	Title I Services Received		Nutrition Programs	Students Receive		Transportation		E-rate 2016	E-rate 2017
	Schools	Students	Schools	Breakfast	Lunch	Schools	Students	Schools Received	Schools Applied
BAKER	0	16	0	0	32	0	0	1	1
PORTLAND	26	476	14	673	692	2	117	12	11
TEXAS	**151**	**5,204**	**66**	**2,411**	**3,746**	**2**	**54**	**166**	**164**
AMARILLO	4	127	2	0	68	0	0	0	0
AUSTIN	9	167	5	0	198	0	0	21	19
BEAUMONT	4	617	0	0	0	0	0	3	3
BROWNSVILLE	10	533	3	330	330	0	0	5	5
CORPUS CHRISTI	9	367	6	246	260	0	0	2	2
DALLAS	18	628	3	393	450	0	0	33	33
EL PASO	9	255	8	252	475	1	26	11	10
FORT WORTH	12	441	7	0	439	1	28	1	1
GALVESTON-HOUSTON	31	805	10	753	753	0	0	44	43
LAREDO	5	88	0	0	0	0	0	7	6
LUBBOCK	2	2	0	0	0	0	0	0	0
SAN ANGELO	1	12	0	0	0	0	0	0	0
SAN ANTONIO	22	787	14	437	604	0	0	26	29
TYLER	3	62	0	0	0	0	0	3	3
VICTORIA	12	313	8	0	169	0	0	10	10
UTAH	**6**	**135**	**0**	**127**	**376**	**1**	**34**	**4**	**5**
SALT LAKE CITY	6	135	0	127	376	1	34	4	5
WASHINGTON	**53**	**848**	**27**	**313**	**882**	**10**	**156**	**12**	**42**
SEATTLE	41	596	23	207	617	8	136	5	34
SPOKANE	7	109	0	43	92	0	0	5	5
YAKIMA	5	143	4	63	173	2	20	2	3
WYOMING	**7**	**154**	**7**	**50**	**129**	**0**	**0**	**1**	**2**
CHEYENNE	7	154	7	50	129	0	0	1	2
WEST/FAR WEST	**685**	**24,014**	**423**	**19,530**	**32,393**	**20**	**639**	**660**	**705**
Grand Total:	**3,466**	**113,675**	**2,971**	**122,538**	**209,401**	**1,933**	**221,366**	**3,084**	**3,321**

References

Broughman, S.P.,and Swaim, N.L. (2016). *Characteristics of Private Schools in the United States: Results From the 2013–14 Private School Universe Survey* (NCES 2016-243). U.S. Department of Education. Washington, DC: National Center for Education Statistics. Retrieved 1/6/2017 from http://nces.ed.gov/pubsearch

Cornman, S.Q., and Zhou, L. (2016). *Revenues and Expenditures for Public Elementary and Secondary Education: School Year 2013–14 (Fiscal Year 2014)* (NCES 2016-301). National Center for Education Statistics, U.S. Department of Education. Washington, DC. Retrieved 1/27/2017 from http://nces.ed.gov/pubsearch.

Glander, M. (2016). *Selected Statistics From the Public Elementary and Secondary Education Universe: School Year 2014-15* (NCES 2016-076) U.S. Department of Education. Washington, DC: National Center for Education Statistics. Retrieved 1/30/2017 from http://nces.ed.gov/pubsearch.

Kena, G., Hussar W., McFarland J., de Brey C., Musu-Gillette, L., Wang, X., Zhang, J., Rathbun, A., Wilkinson-Flicker, S., Diliberti M., Barmer, A., Bullock Mann, F., and Dunlop Velez, E. (2016). *The Condition of Education 2016* (NCES 2016-144). U.S. Department of Education, National Center for Education Statistics. Washington, DC. Retrieved 1/30/2017 from http://nces.ed.gov/pubsearch

Kramarek, M.J., Gray, M.M., and McDonald, D. (2016). *The Annual Financial Report: Catholic Elementary and Secondary Schools in the United States: 2015-2016.* Arlington, VA: National Catholic Educational Association.

McDonald, D., and Schultz, M. (2012). *United States Catholic Elementary and Secondary Schools 2011-2012.* Arlington, VA: National Catholic Educational Association.